me and my sewing machine

a beginner's guide

Kate Haxell

APPLE

First published in the UK in 2010
by
Apple Press
7 Greenland Street
London NW1 0ND
United Kingdom

www.apple-press.com

Photography Dominic Harris
Design Louise Leffler

This book was conceived and
produced by Breslich & Foss Ltd
Unit 2a Union Court
20–22 Union Road
London SW4 6JP

A CIP catalogue record for
this book is available from the
British Library.

ISBN 978 1 84543 353 6

Printed and bound in China

10 9 8 7 6 5 4 3 2 1

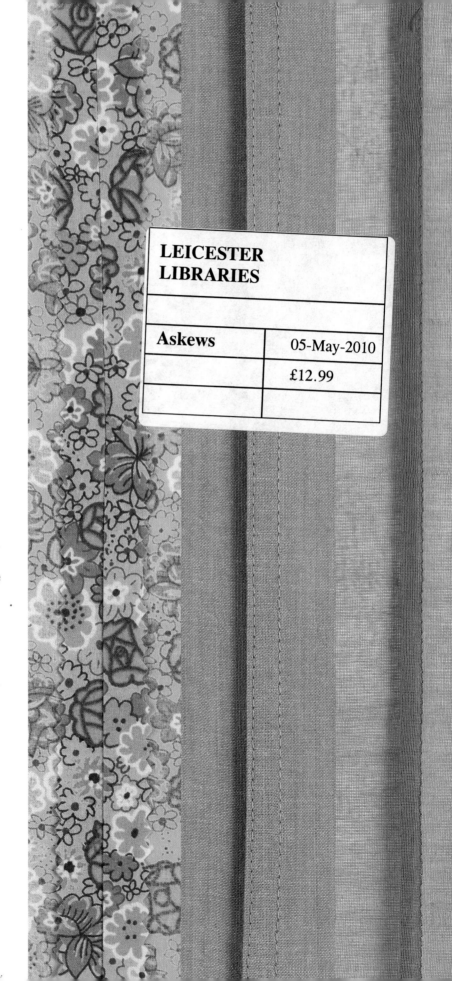

CONTENTS

Introduction

Turning a piece of flat fabric into a three-dimensional item that is both useful and beautiful is the most extraordinarily satisfying pastime. You have bought this book (or some lovely person has given it to you) because you, too, want that satisfaction, and so I'm delighted to welcome you to the truly global sewing circle.

I don't remember my first stitches, though I do remember sitting cross-legged in primary school sewing something or another: the unfortunate Julia Lloyd stitched right through her project and sewed it to her skirt. I earned pocket money sewing name labels into all of my three brothers' school clothes, even their socks. I was paid (with hindsight, rather poorly) by the label and both my mother (who didn't love sewing) and I were happy.

My skills have progressed since then, learned piecemeal from better sewers, from magazines, from getting it wrong the first time and from books. However, I've always found the vast sewing tomes rather off-putting. There's just such a huge amount of information: am I expected to know it all? What on earth for? So this is a different kind of sewing book. From what to look for when buying your sewing machine, through the practicalities of seams, hems and fastenings, to the decorative delights of ruffles, pleats and ribbons, this book contains information and techniques you need to know to sew well using your sewing machine – and nothing more.

There are no scary couture-type techniques that real sewers never use, no painstaking procedures that don't actually make your sewing easier – or help it look better – and no complicated methods of doing anything. Instead, you will find step-by-step methods that make sewing simple, even if you have never used a machine before.

I hope that you and your sewing machine become the best of friends and that you revel in the world it opens up for you.

Kate Haxell

My sewing machine

A sewing machine doesn't have to be an expensive purchase these days: you can buy a basic, inexpensive new machine or hunt on internet auction sites for a bargain. If you decide to do the latter, do take as much care as possible to ensure that what you are buying is all it seems to be.

How a sewing machine works

Nearly all modern sewing machines work in basically the same way. There will be variations in the way the bobbin goes in, the way you thread the top spool and the way you select functions, but the underlying principles will be similar.

You certainly don't need a detailed technical explanation of how all machines do everything, but some information is useful – so here are some photographs of my sewing machine with captions telling you what is what.

In the manual that comes with your sewing machine there should be photographs like these ones, or diagrams, that tell you about that particular machine. If you don't have a manual, contact the machine's manufacturer and see if they can send you one, or check on the internet to see if there is one you can download. Alternatively, if you have a friendly local sewing shop, take your machine in and ask them to explain it to you.

Side view

handwheel: turn this to manually raise or lower the needle

power switch

power socket: where the foot pedal – which makes the machine run – is plugged in

Front view

spool thread take-up lever: the sewing thread goes through here as well

spool thread guide: the sewing thread goes through here to thread up the machine

bobbin winder thread guide: the sewing thread goes through here when you are filling a bobbin

selected stitch

thread spool pin: this is where you put the reel of thread you are going to sew with

range of stitches available

bobbin winder spindle: this is where you put the empty bobbin to fill it with thread

second thread spool pin: you can sew with two threads

bobbin winder stopper: this stops the bobbin overfilling

thread tension dial: turn this to adjust the thread tension (see Tension, page 12)

stitch length selector

stitch width and, depending on the pattern selected, needle position

handwheel: turn this to manually raise or lower the needle

thread cutter

needle threader

needle

stitch selector dial

presser foot lifter: for raising and lowering the presser foot

reverse stitch lever: for sewing backwards

needle clamp

bobbin housing

Needle, presser foot and throat plate

one-step buttonhole lever

needle threader: a useful optional feature if you struggle to thread fine needles

presser foot holder

needle

feed dogs: these feed the fabric under the needle at a rate controlled by how hard you press the power pedal

needle clamp: this holds the needle in the machine

presser foot: this is lowered to sit on top of the fabric. There are different feet for different sewing tasks

throat plate with measurements marked

Hook race and bobbin case

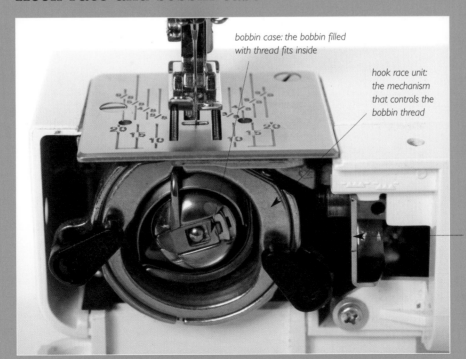

bobbin case: the bobbin filled with thread fits inside

hook race unit: the mechanism that controls the bobbin thread

feed dog drop lever: for dropping the feed dogs to do free-motion embroidery

Tension

All sewers, novices and skilled seamstresses alike, sometimes wonder if the machine's tension is what is causing their tension. Incorrect thread tension is probably the most common sewing problem and it can completely ruin a project.

The first thing to understand is what sewing machine tension actually is. The term 'tension' refers to the amount of pressure on the sewing thread coming from the top reel. This pressure is exerted by the tension discs, which are inside the machine and through which the sewing thread passes when you thread up the machine.

Different fabrics and stitches need different amounts of tension. The tension is controlled by the thread tension dial on the front of the machine (see page 10). Turning the dial to a higher number increases the tension and to a lower number, decreases it. On most machines,

turning the dial to number 5 will give you a tension suitable for straight stitch on mediumweight fabric.

If the bobbin thread is visible on the right side of the fabric or the spool thread is visible on the wrong side, then the tension is not set correctly. Also, if seams are puckered, the thread keeps breaking, knotting or jamming the machine, or stitches are getting skipped, then incorrect tension could be the cause.

Before you start a project, always test the tension on a scrap of the project fabric. Fold it double to check how seams will sew; if you are using lining or interfacing, add a scrap of that; test the stitches you are planning to use. Duplicate all aspects of the project in miniature and get the tension right – this really is worth the time and effort. If you skip this testing then any tension problems can spoil your project.

Balanced tension

If the tension is set properly, then the bobbin and spool threads interlock within the layers of fabric, as above. Only the spool thread is visible on the right side and only the bobbin thread on the wrong side.

Top tension too loose

If the spool thread is visible on the wrong side, then the top tension is too loose. Try sewing a line of stitching with a reel of contrast thread on the spool pin. Dots of the contrast colour on the wrong side will tell you that the top tension needs increasing. Turn the dial to a half number higher and sew a test, as before.

Top tension too tight

If the bobbin thread is visible on the right side, then the top tension is too tight. If you are unsure as to whether this is the problem, put a contrast colour thread on the bobbin and sew a line of stitching on a scrap of the project fabric. If you can see dots of the contrast colour on the fabric, then the top tension is indeed too tight. Turn the thread tension dial to a half number lower and sew another line. Continue decreasing the tension by half a number until it is balanced.

A tension test

Sew a line diagonally across a square of fabric, so that the stitching is on the bias (see Making Bias Strip and Binding, pages 74–75). Hold the ends of the stitched line firmly and pull hard so the fabric stretches. If only the top thread breaks, then the top tension is too tight. If only the bottom thread breaks, then the top tension is too loose. If both threads break, then the tension is balanced.

More tension issues

If you've adjusted the tension dial but are still having problems, then check the following as they may be affecting tension.

Have you threaded the machine correctly, top and bottom? Pull the top thread out and thread it up again. If the machine is new, check the manual to make sure you're not missing out a stage. Take out the bobbin and re-insert it, again checking that you are doing it properly.

How long have you been using the needle? If you've been sewing with the same needle for some time then it might be blunt or bent. Just pulling on the fabric can bend a needle and the tiniest defect can cause problems. Change the needle, making sure you select the right one for the fabric (see pages 22–23). In fact, you should change the needle regularly: 'new project, new needle' is a good motto.

Is the machine clean? As you sew, lint from the fabrics builds up in the machine. If you don't clean it regularly then the hook race and bobbin case (see page 11) can get clogged with lint and this will cause sewing chaos. A little brush for cleaning out these components should have come with the machine, so use it.

What kind of thread are you using? If you are sewing with a cheap thread you picked up in a market, then try swapping it for a good-quality, brand-name thread (see Threads, page 23).

Are you using a plastic bobbin? If you are, is it elderly? Nicks in the rim of a bobbin, even tiny ones, can catch the thread. Swap the bobbin for a new one and see if that cures the problem.

The other tension

The bobbin case also has a tension adjustment, but you should only use it if you really can't fix the problem by adjusting the top tension and you have checked that thread, needle or lint issues aren't the cause of the trouble.

Usually, you would only expect to adjust the bobbin case tension if you were using a thick or decorative thread on the bobbin. Machine embroiderers, who often do use fancy bobbin threads, may have two bobbin cases; one that is never adjusted and is used for ordinary sewing and one for their fancy threads, which is fiddled with at will.

To alter the bobbin case tension, you use a special screwdriver (which should be supplied with your machine) to turn the tiny screw in the bobbin case. Turn it to the left to decrease the tension and to the right to increase the tension. Hold the bobbin case over an empty box while you do this, because if the tiny screw falls out it's very difficult to find again.

Make a note of the direction you turned the screw in and how far you turned it so that you can re-set the tension to the factory setting when or if you need to.

Buying your first sewing machine

The first step in buying your own sewing machine is to decide which functions you are going to need. Modern sewing machines range from very basic models that do little more than sew straight lines, to computerised machines with a myriad of features to make your head spin. You are almost certainly going to want something in between.

For a first sewing machine you need a model that is simple enough to use easily and yet sophisticated enough to grow into. You won't want to spend too much on your first machine, just in case you decide sewing's not the craft for you, but bear in mind that a really cheap machine may not sew very well.

I recommend choosing a mid-range machine from a good brand name. This way you get a decent machine and you'll be able to buy extra accessories: the big brands produce wide ranges of these. Most manufacturers are sensible and accessories produced for one machine will fit their other models. So when you upgrade your machine, stay with the same brand and you don't have to buy everything again.

Sewing machines of this type will have the basic straight and zigzag stitches plus some extras, which are all you'll need. One function I do recommend you look for is an automatic, one-step buttonhole. Doing buttonholes manually on the sewing machine is perfectly possible, but doing them automatically is less stressful, quicker and usually better-looking (see pages 58–59).

Another useful feature is a variable needle position: this makes it easier to sew straight lines in odd places as you can align the fabric with a throat plate guide or the edge of the presser foot and then move the needle across to sew in the required spot.

If possible, borrow a machine for a few days and have a good play with it. Check out all the functions and see what you think will be most useful. If you are lucky enough to have a local sewing shop that is not dedicated to one brand of sewing machine, then it's certainly worth asking the staff for recommendations. Otherwise, spend some time browsing the internet and compare reviews.

Sewing machine accessories

Your sewing machine will come with some accessories and to start with you won't need to buy more. As you develop your skills and master new techniques, you'll find some of the items shown useful, though you should buy them as and when you need them. Depending on the make of sewing machine you buy, its presser feet may not look exactly like the ones shown, but they'll do the same things.

Straight foot

This foot is for sewing simple straight lines (see Sewing Straight Lines, page 30), and so is the one you'll use most of the time.

Zigzag foot

The foot you'll use for zigzag stitch and for some automatic decorative stitches (see Stitches, page 23).

Zip foot

These vary a lot in style, but they are all designed to let you stitch as close to the zip teeth as possible (see pages 52–57 for different types of zips).

Patchwork foot

The right-hand toe of this foot is 5mm (¼ in.) wide, so it's useful as a guide for narrow seams. I don't do much patchwork (see Patchwork, page 94), but I use this foot quite a lot.

Clear view foot

This is useful for appliqué because you can easily see what you are doing (see Appliqué, page 93). This one has a recess underneath that allows it to pass smoothly over a line of satin stitch.

Teflon foot

A super-smooth foot that glides over 'sticky' fabrics, such as vinyl.

Blind hem foot

The adjustable right-hand toe lets you set the hem to the required depth (see Blind-stitch Hem, page 44).

Free-motion embroidery foot

This is another foot that varies a lot in style. The open-toe versions, like this one, let you easily see what you are doing (see Free-motion Embroidery, page 92).

Walking foot

This foot helps to feed layers of fabric evenly through the machine when quilting (see Quilting, page 95). They are usually expensive and not always necessary for simple quilting projects.

Automatic buttonhole foot

You fit the button in place and the buttonhole is sewn to the correct size to fit it (see Automatic Buttonhole, page 58).

Sewing machine needles

Picking the right needle for the fabric you are using will make a real difference to your sewing. Shown here, left to right: 8/60, 12/80, 18/110, twin needle, 11/75 embroidery needle, 12/80 metallic thread needle, 14/90 leather needle, 12/80 ballpoint needle.

For advice on which needle to use with which fabric, turn to Fabrics, Threads and Stitches, pages 22–23.

Quilting guide

This fits onto the presser foot to help you sew evenly spaced lines (see Quilting, page 95).

Magnetic guide

This clamps onto the throat plate to help you sew straight lines (see Sewing Straight Lines, page 30).

Sewing tools and equipment

As well as the basics – such as scissors – here are numerous tools and gadgets you can buy to help you with your sewing. These are items I have bought and actually use, as opposed to pieces that live undisturbed in the box they came in.

I have five different pairs of scissors in my workbox, of which you'll need three: fabric shears, embroidery scissors and paper scissors. In addition I have pinking shears and thread snips. I don't buy expensive scissors, but I do take care of them and never use my fabric scissors for cutting paper – it's a sure way to dull the edges of the blades.

Fabric shears
There are different styles available, but ones like these with a bent handle make cutting out fabric easy.

Embroidery scissors
Look for ones with very sharp points and short, slim blades.

Thread snips
I find these very useful for quickly and easily trimming thread ends while machining.

Seam ripper
This is designed for cutting out seams that have gone wrong. Slip the long toe under the stitches and gently push to cut through the thread.

Thimble
This is used for pushing a hand-sewing needle through thick fabric. I prefer rubber thimbles to metal ones.

Pins
I use very long, fine pins with glass heads that can be ironed over without melting. The length and slimness means that they don't mark fabrics and make minimal ripples. I always use magnetic pincushions (this one was designed to be a paperclip holder). Although they do magnetise the pins, they are very convenient.

Hand-sewing needle
You'll sometimes need one of these for finishing off bits of projects. The larger the size number, the finer the needle is.

Whatever measuring system you use – metric or imperial – stick to it and don't chop and change between the two or you'll end up in a measuring mess. This book has both styles of measurement for every technique and project.

Seam gauge
I use this all the time for measuring short distances, such as for hems and seams. Set the red slider to the required distance and it's quick and easy to measure and check.

Cloth tape measure
This is indispensable; wear it draped around your neck to feel like a true seamstress.

Long and short rules
These are useful, but not essential, though mine do have a permanent home in my workbox.

There are various fabric markers available. The two types I use are a water-soluble marker and tailor's chalk. Air-soluble markers are good, but I find that too often the mark has disappeared before I've finished the project. Whichever marker you use, always test it on a scrap of the fabric first to ensure it will completely disappear.

Bias binding maker
A great bit of kit for making your own bias binding.

Bobbin ring
A neat piece of equipment for storing bobbins, items that otherwise end up in a tangled mess in your workbox.

Water-soluble fabric marker
Remember that water can mark fabrics, so when you test the marker on the fabric, wet it and iron it dry to check that no watermarks appear.

Tailor's chalk
The classic fabric marker, the chalk easily brushes off most fabrics.

Getting ready to sew

There are a few basic bits of knowledge and some general skills that you'll find useful for whichever techniques in this book you are going to tackle. Read this chapter through before you launch into any sewing – it's worth it.

A space for sewing

The vast majority of home sewers don't have the luxury of a dedicated sewing room and instead have to make do with space stolen from the guest bedroom or a corner of the living room. However, a small space can be perfectly effective if you organise it well.

You are going to need a sturdy table, a comfortable, straight-back chair and an iron and ironing board close by. If you have the iron in another room you may not want to get up and go to press the fabric when you should and your sewing will suffer as a result (see Pressing, pages 26–27). In an ideal world the table will be big enough to cut out fabric on as well as hold the sewing machine. If this isn't possible, then you can cut out on the floor – make sure it's clean first.

Sewers, like knitters, quite quickly build up a stash. Delicious fabrics, gorgeous trimmings, colourful threads and lovely buttons are irresistible, and can take up a surprisingly large amount of space. If you don't organise them properly then you'll never be able to find the prefect piece when you need it. You'll go out and buy another and your stash will just grow and grow, full of many similar things.

I like to use see-through storage as much as possible: I keep small pieces of fabric folded in clear plastic, stackable crates and I store buttons by colour in plastic button tubes. Larger pieces of fabric are folded in a cupboard, organised by fibre. Ribbons and trimmings are wound and clipped with mini wooden clothes pegs (originally sold as office stationery, though I don't know what you are supposed to do with them in that context).

An excellent way to store sewing spools of thread is on a DIY rack (see below left): mine is mounted on the outside of a cupboard door as I think the threads are so decorative. To make a spool rack, you hammer nails into strips of wooden moulding then screw the moulding to the door. Slip the cotton reels onto the nails, arranging them by colour for best effect. If you're more of a shopper than a DIYer, then you can buy ready-made wooden spool racks.

A capacious workbox – but not too big to carry – to hold all your sewing machine accessories and other bits of sewing kit is a must. I use a mechanic's toolbox as it has fold-out trays and lots of space, but there are many dedicated sewing boxes available.

It doesn't really matter how you organise and store your stash and equipment as long as you know where things are and can get to them easily. Inefficient storage is almost as bad as no storage at all.

How to run a sewing machine

Once you have got your new sewing machine home, the very first thing to do is to read the manual. Even if you have used a sewing machine before, different makes and models have different operating details and, if you don't read the instructions, you can end up damaging your machine before you've finished your first sewing project.

Set up the machine on a sturdy table. A decorator's folding table, or even a gate-leg table, are not good choices because when a machine is running at full pelt it can bounce to an alarming degree if the table isn't solid, and that really will ruin your sewing. Pull up a straight-back, armless chair – a dining chair is good, but not a wheeled office chair as they move too easily – and check that the machine is at the right height for you to operate it comfortably. Can you reach the power pedal easily without stretching your leg? Is the power cable safely out of the way and not stretched tightly to the machine so that if you trip over it you'll pull the machine off the table? Is the machine high enough for you to see the fabric going under the needle without craning your neck? But low enough for you to sew without having to lift your arms uncomfortably high? All ok? Excellent!

With the manual read, the machine set up, a medium straight stitch selected and a piece of fabric to experiment with chosen, you are ready to start sewing. The first thing to do is to sew a line, check the stitch tension and adjust it if necessary (see Tension, page 12).

Then you need to get your hands in the right position. Novice sewers sometimes hold the fabric as shown above right, with one hand clutching the front edge and the other at the back pulling the fabric through. This is not how to sew. The feed dogs (see page 11) feed the fabric through the machine at a rate controlled by how hard you press the power pedal; you don't need to help them do their job.

Pulling the fabric like this is also an easy way to bend the needle. Needles are only slivers of metal and they bend easily, and then you can have all sorts of tension problems (see Tension, page 12).

Your job is to guide the fabric so that it passes under the needle where you want the stitching to be. To this end, have both hands resting lightly on the fabric, fairly flat and quite close to the presser foot, as shown below right. Obviously you want to avoid sewing your fingers, but that is reasonably easy to do. NEVER take your eyes off the needle when it's moving. If someone calls you, stop sewing, then look up. Don't sew in front of the television where you'll be tempted to glance at the action on screen.

Position the fabric under the presser foot with the edge against one of the marks on the throat plate (see Sewing Straight Lines, page 30). Get comfortable in your chair and put your hands on the fabric. GENTLY press the power pedal. As the fabric runs under the needle and away from you, keep moving your hands so that they stay in the same position in relation to the needle and gently steer the fabric so that the edge of it stays against the same mark on the throat plate.

Get used to how the fabric moves under the needle, then press the pedal a little harder. Sew back and forth across the piece of fabric, changing speeds and stitch patterns until you are comfortable sewing: this may take more than one session. However, it's well worth continuing to experiment and practise on non-lovely fabric until you are really confident with your machine before starting a project. If you are still at the practice stage, any project will suffer and you'll be discouraged and that's never good.

The wrong way to hold the fabric when sewing.

The right way to steer the fabric when sewing.

Fabrics, threads and stitches

There is an absolutely huge range of fabrics available to today's sewer, far too huge a range to discuss in detail here. On these pages there is an overview of the most popular sewing fabrics, plus a little advice on threads and stitches.

Fabrics

There'll usually be two main reasons why you choose a fabric for a project; one is practical – how suitable the fabric is – and one is aesthetic – how much you like the fabric. Try not to choose a fabric solely for the second reason, as it could mean that your project just doesn't work out no matter how carefully you sew.

Left, from the top the fabrics in this pile are:

Lace Most modern lace fabrics are made from man-made fibres, though you can buy gorgeous, and expensive, silk and cotton lace. Lace is mainly used for bridal and evening gowns, overlaid on another fabric. It isn't especially difficult to sew, though very delicate and vintage lace can be fragile. Use a fine needle from a 60/8 to an 75/11.

Lining fabric Generally made from synthetic fibres, lining materials come in a myriad of solid colours and great patterns. I love using fancy lining; even if no one else sees it, you know it is there and it makes a garment that bit more special. Linings are slippery and can be really tricky to sew, so I recommend tacking (see Tacking, page 25). For real luxury, you can buy silk lining fabric that feels wonderful next to your skin. Sew synthetic lining with an 75/11 or a 80/12 needle and silk lining with an 75/11 or finer.

Tweed This is a traditional Irish wool tweed and is thick and heavy – ideal for a warm winter coat. It's easy enough to sew, though as it's such a chunky weave it does fray quite easily. Sew it with a 90/14 or 100/16 needle.

Silk This is dupion silk, which is probably the easiest silk fabric to sew as it's the least slippery. However, it frays madly, marks easily and will shift around given the chance. Having said that, silk looks and feels so lovely that it's hard to resist for a special dress. Tack your seams (see Tacking, page 25), finish all raw edges (see Finishing Edges, page 32), and be very careful of watermarks when pressing (see Pressing, pages 26–27). Sew silk with an 75/11 needle or finer.

Suedette A fake suede fabric made from synthetic fibres, this comes in a limited range of colours. It's not the easiest fabric to sew because, like velvet, when two layers are right sides facing they try to 'creep' along one another and create an uneven seam. Firm, short-stitch tacking (see Tacking, page 25) will help keep this fabric under control. Lightweight suedette can be sewn with a 80/12 or 90/14 needle. For heavier suedettes (and real suede) use a 90/14 or 100/16 leather needle.

Wool Versatile, available in different weights, colours and patterns, and easy to sew, wool is a wonderful fabric. Be careful pressing it (see Pressing, pages 26–27), as too much heat and steam can felt the surface. Sew lightweight wools with a 80/12 needle, moving up to a 100/16 for the heaviest weights.

Printed cotton The most popular sewing fabric in the world. You can buy cotton fabric in almost any colour and design you could want, and it has many different names. Do check the fibre content on 'cotton' fabrics as they can have a man-made fibre mixed in, which you may or may not want. Remember that with large-scale patterns you may want to pattern-match at the seams, so you'll need to buy extra fabric and tack the seams (see Tacking, page 25). Generally easy to sew, choose an 75/11 needle for the lightest weight cottons – such as chambray – going up to a 110/18 for thick cotton duck. Mediumweight dressmaking cotton can be sewn with a 80/12.

Satin Often made from synthetic fibres, satin can be lovely to look at and really horrid to sew. It slips, shifts around, marks at the first possible opportunity and often doesn't press well. If you're absolutely set on using satin, tack (see Tacking, page 25) everything within the seam allowances and sew with an 75/11 needle.

Velvet This is velvet with a crushed finish, which does make this a slightly more forgiving fabric than straight-pile velvet. However, velvet is for experienced sewers only: it's probably the most difficult fabric there is to sew beautifully. You need to tack every seam using the long-and-short technique (see Tacking, page 25), ideally sew it with a walking foot (see Sewing Machine Accessories, page 14), and press the fabric on a special needleboard with paper under the seam allowances to stop them making an impression on the right side. And velvet frays like nothing else on earth. If you really, really must have velvet, then sew it with great care and a 80/12 or 90/14 needle.

Solid-colour cotton All the attributes of printed cotton with none of the pattern-matching issues. Perfect!

Corduroy Usually made from cotton – sometimes with synthetic fibre mixed in – corduroy is hardwearing and fairly easy to sew. In a similar way to velvet, the furry finish can 'creep' a little when you are sewing two pieces right sides together, so tacking (see Tacking, page 25) is a good idea. Use a 90/14 needle to sew corduroy.

Threads

The golden rule for threads is not to buy cheap ones. They'll usually be poor quality, will snap, fray and there won't be very much on the spool so you'll run out quickly.

To avoid potential laundering complications, sew fabrics with thread made of the same fibre whenever you can. So, use cotton thread for cottons, silk thread for silks and polyester thread for man-made fibres and for woollen fabrics, as there is no such thing as wool thread.

Rayon and metallic threads are generally used for machine embroidery (see Free-motion Embroidery, page 92) and should be sewn with a metallic or embroidery needle, which have a very sharp point and an elongated eye to help them pierce the fabric smoothly and easily.

Stitches

Basic manual machines might offer fewer than ten different stitches, while the computerised sewing machines can produce dozens of fancy stitches, so we can't look at everything here. However, most of the time you'll only use a few stitches and we can look at those.

Below, from the left these stitches are:
Straight stitch There are three different stitch lengths shown here. A very short stitch, a medium stitch – the one you'll usually use – and a long stitch that's used for gathering and machine tacking.

Stretch straight stitch This is a more elastic version of straight stitch and should be used to sew stretchy woven and knit fabrics.

Zigzag stitch Used to finish edges (see Finishing Edges, page 32), this stitch can be set to different widths and tightness.

Satin stitch This is a wide, tight zigzag stitch used for edging appliqué motifs (see Appliqué, page 93).

Tricot stitch This is the version of zigzag stitch that you use to finish the edges (see Finishing Edges, page 32) of stretchy fabrics.

Overcast stitch Another stitch that's used to finish edges (see Finishing Edges, page 32).

Box stitch Used to join pieces of wadding for quilting (see Quilting, page 95). Overlap the edges of the wadding by 1cm (⅜ in.) and sew a line of box stitch along the overlap for a smooth, non-bulky join.

Embroidery stitches The last two stitches are automatic embroidery stitches. These can offer a quick and easy way of adding detail to a project.

Pinning

Putting pins in pieces of fabric to hold them together may not sound like it needs any instructions, but there are a couple of tricks that'll make your machine-sewing easier and help prevent you pricking yourself more often than absolutely necessary.

Pinning for machine-sewing

Pin like this and you'll never have the annoyance of the head of the pin facing the needle as you sew towards it, making it difficult to take out.

Match the edges of the fabrics to be joined and have the raw edge facing away from you. If it's a hem, fold the edge up and have the fold facing away from you. Starting at the point where you'll start sewing, put in pins with the heads facing to the right. As you sew the seam the heads will all face you, ready to be easily pulled out before the needle reaches them.

Pinning for tacking

If you're pinning prior to tacking, then do it like this to avoid pricking yourself as you sew.

Match the edges of the fabrics to be joined and have the raw edge facing towards you. If it's a hem, fold the edge up and have the fold facing towards you. Starting at the end of the seam nearest you, the point where you'll start tacking, put the pins in with the heads facing to the right. As you tack towards them the heads, not the points, of the pins will be facing you.

Pinning pattern pieces

Pinning paper patterns to fabric needs to be done carefully and well to make sure that the piece of fabric you cut out is in fact the same shape as the paper pattern piece.

Firstly, make sure the fabric is smooth and flat. If it has wrinkles or folds, press them out (see Pressing, pages 26–27). Lay the pattern piece on the fabric and smooth it flat with your hands: if it's very wrinkled, then iron it with a warm, dry iron. Put in lots of pins, making sure that all points and valleys are held to the fabric. The full length of each pin must be within the pattern piece so that you don't nick the blades of your fabric scissors when you cut around the paper.

Sewing over pins

My grandma, who taught me to sew, didn't hold with this and I never do it, but other sewers I know do. I include the technique here, but if you're going to use it, do so with caution.

Match the edges of the fabrics to be joined and put the pins in at right angles to the raw edge, leaving the heads protruding. Sew the seam fairly slowly, sewing over the shafts of the pins. Take the pins out once the stitching is complete.

The reasons I don't hold with sewing over pins are firstly that you quite often hit a pin with the needle, at best making an irregular stitch and at worst breaking the needle. Pins can wrinkle the fabric if they're not placed properly and then you sew the wrinkle into the seam. Finally, if the fabrics need holding together while you sew then it really doesn't take long to tack them.

Cutting out

Accurate cutting is essential for accurate sewing. The aim is to cut the fabric while keeping it as flat as possible on the work surface: lifting the fabric almost guarantees wobbly cut edges.

Fabric scissors with bent handles allow the blades to cut close to and parallel to the work surface, lifting the fabric only a little, without your having to contort your hand into an odd position.

Open the blades as wide as is comfortable for your hand and slip the lower blade under the fabric where you want to start cutting. Close the blades smoothly, cutting the fabric, but do not close them fully. Just before the tips of the blades close, open them wide again and slide the lower blade further under the fabric along the cutting line. Cutting this way (without fully closing the blades) will help avoid snags and dips in the cut edge.

Tacking

In today's hurry-along world, anything that takes a little more time is often cast aside whether or not it's useful, and tacking can be so very useful. I'm not saying you should *always* tack, but for slippery fabrics, shaped seams, trimmings and neat zips, pinning and hoping won't usually be enough.

Seams and hems

For seams or hems in fabrics that aren't inherently tricky to sew (see Fabrics, page 22), you only need to tack if the seam is shaped or the hem is curved.

Pin the fabric along the tacking line (see Pinning for Tacking, opposite). Thread a slim needle with thread the length of the line to be tacked plus 15cm (6 in.). If this is ridiculously long and impossible to use, then you'll need to tack the line in two sections.

Sew a line of running stitch, with stitches about 1cm (⅜ in.) long, along the tacking line.

The tacking line doesn't need to be measured and marked, as it doesn't matter if it is a bit wobbly. The stitches don't have to be neat and even, though they should be firm and not too long or they won't do their job.

Slippery fabrics and fabrics with pile – such as velvet – should always be tacked and it's best to use the long-and-short technique. This involves making firm stitches that vary in length between 5mm (¼ in.) and 1cm (⅜ in.): the irregularity in stitch length helps to keep the layers of fabric from shifting.

Taking the needle in and out of the fabric to put several stitches on it before pulling the thread through, as shown here, is a quick and perfectly valid way of tacking a seam or hem. However, when putting in a zip or tacking a tricky corner, you may well find it better to make individual stitches.

Where to tack

One of the most common mistakes novice sewers make is to tack precisely where the line of machine-sewing will be. They then have to spend time picking out the tacking stitches without damaging the machine stitches.

So, whenever possible, tack a little distance from where you will machine-sew. For a seam with a standard 1.5cm (⅝ in.) seam allowance, tack about 1cm (⅜ in.) from the edge of the fabric. If you are machining a hem and will have the edge of the presser foot against the fold, then tack right next to the fold.

Pressing

When you're making a sewing project, you should be using your iron almost as much as your sewing machine. Proper, accurate pressing will make the most enormous difference to your sewing, on both a practical and an aesthetic level.

The practicalities of pressing

There is a difference between pressing and ironing. Ironing involves moving the iron around on the fabric and is what you do to freshly laundered garments. Pressing involves placing the iron in one spot, then lifting it and placing it in another, without dragging on the fabric.

If at all possible, set up your iron and ironing board in the room you sew in (see A Space For Sewing, page 20). You should press your project every time you sew a section of it and if the iron is to hand and you don't have to leave the room, then you are more likely to be good about doing this.

Check what temperature your fabric can be pressed at. Generally, cotton and linen can be pressed with a hot iron, wool with a warm iron and synthetics with a cool iron. However, this isn't a firm rule and introducing steam can change things, so you need to test a scrap of fabric first to check that you have the right temperature.

Before using steam on a fabric, check that any watermarks you might make on the fabric will disappear. Drop a little water on to a scrap of the fabric and iron it dry, then check that no watermark remains. Steam has two functions: it helps take out very stubborn folds and creases and it will 'set' fabric into a shape. How firm the 'set' will be depends on the fabric, and it will lose its shape when washed and then need re-pressing. Most irons have a steam function and will produce different amounts of steam at different temperatures. Alternatively, spray the fabric with water using a spray bottle and then press it to create steam, or use a dampened pressing cloth.

My favourite pressing cloth is an old cotton tea towel with the hems cut off to prevent them making impressions on the fabric. A piece of silk organza can be a useful pressing cloth as its translucency enables you to see what you are doing, but it needs frequent dampening.

My favourite cotton pressing cloth.

An organza pressing cloth.

Pressing seams

'Press seam open' is a common instruction in sewing books and involves laying the fabric flat, opening out the seam allowances (see Sewing Straight Lines, page 30), and pressing them flat against the wrong side of the fabric.

1.

2.

1 The first stage in pressing a seam open is to press it flat. Without opening out the fabric, press over the line of stitching you have just done to help the stitches sink into the fabric.

2 Then open the fabric out and lay it flat, right side down. Open out the seam allowances and press them flat. Turn the fabric over and check that the edges of the allowances haven't made an imprint on the fabric. If they have, then you need to slip strips of paper under the seam allowances and press them again.

Tailor's ham

This is a small, very firm cushion that you can lay a curved seam over (see Inward Curve and Outward Curve, pages 68–69) so that you can press it open without pressing it flat at the same time. It's a really useful piece of equipment. You can buy a ham, but it's easy to make your own.

1 Lay your iron on a piece of dressmaking cotton fabric and draw around it. Curve out the sides a little and round off the corners to make a classic ham shape, then add 5cm (2 in.) all around.

2 Cut out the shape and use this as a template to cut the same shape once in woollen fabric and twice in thick cotton. Lay out a thick cotton ham shape with the dressmaking cotton shape face up on top of it, then the woollen shape face down and finally the other thick cotton shape. Pin the layers together.

3 Set the sewing machine to a medium straight stitch. Taking a 1cm (⅜ in.) seam allowance, machine around the edges, leaving a 10cm (4 in.) gap.

4 Turn the ham right side out through the gap. Fill it with sawdust (the type sold as bedding for hamsters is ideal), spooning it through the gap. You need to stuff the ham very firmly indeed, so use the spoon to press the sawdust down inside the ham so that you can force in as much as possible.

5 Hand-sew the gap closed using oversewing stitch to complete the ham. If after a few weeks the sawdust has compacted and the ham feels a bit soft, then you'll need to unpick the gap and push more sawdust in.

6 Lay a curved seam over the ham and press it open. Having one side of the ham in wool and one side in cotton allows you to use a high heat on the cotton side if it's needed.

Pressing sleeves

You can make or buy a sleeve roll, which is a sausage-shaped version of a tailor's ham, but I prefer to use a towel because it can be made to fit any size or length of sleeve.

Roll the towel up so that it slides inside the sleeve, filling it without stretching it. You can now press the sleeve seam open without pressing the sleeve flat. This is also useful when you're ironing if you don't want pressed lines running down your sleeves.

Seams simple

The first and simplest sewing technique to learn is the seam. Once you can sew two pieces of fabric together, you can make something. There are different styles of seam and various ways of finishing the seam allowances, depending on what you are making and the fabric you use.

Sewing straight lines

Most often the seam you require will be straight and it's important that you sew it straight. A wobbly seam will look terrible and can affect the fit of a garment. Many beginners struggle to sew in a straight line, but there are tips and tricks for mastering this and of course I am going to share them with you. The amount of fabric between the raw, cut edge and the line of stitching that makes the seam is called the seam allowance. In dressmaking the standard seam allowance is 1.5cm (⅝ in.), though you should always check a sewing pattern to see what it requires.

Check out...

Sewing tools and equipment,
    pages 16-17
How to run a sewing
    machine, page 21
Stitches, page 23

Plate marks

To help you keep to a straight line when sewing fabric, you can use one of four easy methods. Firstly, on the throat plate of the sewing machine there will be lines at marked distances from the needle, when it is in its usual sewing position. Usually these lines will be at 1cm (⅜ in.), 1.5cm (⅝ in.) and 2cm (¾ in.) from the needle. If you keep the edge of the fabric running along the relevant marked line, the line of stitching will be that distance from the edge, giving you a seam allowance of that width.

Magnetic guide

To make this easier still, you can buy a magnetic seam guide. This is a handy little gadget that you put on the throat plate along the appropriate marked line. It gives you a raised, easy-to-see guide to keep the edge of the fabric running against while you sew the seam.

Masking tape

If you have to sew with a seam allowance that is wider than any of the marks on the throat plate, then stick a piece of masking tape on the bed of the machine to act as a guide. Measure out the required extra distance from the last marked line on the throat plate then stick on the tape, being careful to keep it parallel to the marked line.

Straight lines

Before you start sewing fabric, get some sheets of ruled paper (pages from an ordinary notebook are perfect) and practise sewing along the lines. Set the sewing machine to a medium straight stitch, take it slowly, pressing the foot pedal gently, and get used to guiding the paper with your hands to keep the line of sewing running along a line on the paper.

Before you start sewing fabric you MUST change the needle in the sewing machine because sewing the paper will have made it blunt.

Marked line

A completely different way of keeping to a seam line is to mark it on the fabric. Always use a proper fabric marker and test it on a scrap of the fabric first to make sure that you can remove the mark. This method can be useful when sewing a shaped seam, as you can concentrate on the stitching and not worry about where the edge of the fabric is.

Starting and finishing sewing

You need to secure the ends of all lines of stitching or they will work loose and your seams will split. There are two simple ways of doing this.

Check out...
Stitches, page 23
How to run a sewing machine, page 21
Sewing straight lines, page 30

Reverse stitching

Most modern sewing machines have a reverse stitch function. This is usually a little lever that you hold down, or a button you push, to make the machine sew backwards, and a few backwards stitches are a great way to secure the ends of most seams.

Position the fabric in the machine with the raw edges against the appropriate seam allowance mark and so that the needle will start sewing about 1cm (⅜ in.) from the start of the seam. You can check that the fabric is positioned correctly by turning the handwheel to lower the needle until it just touches the fabric. Hold down the reverse lever and slowly sew a few stitches backwards. Try not to sew over the edge of the fabric as it may pucker.

Release the reverse lever and machine-sew forwards to sew the seam. When you reach the other end of the seam, just before you get to the edge of the fabric, hold down the lever and sew backwards for 1cm (⅜ in.).

Knotting ends

If the line of stitching is visible (for example, topstitching), a reversed end can look untidy. The best solution here is to tie the threads in a firm knot on the wrong side of the fabric.

1 Before starting to sew, pull the top and bobbin threads through the machine until they are about 10cm (4 in.) long. Then sew the seam. At the other end, cut the threads 10cm (4 in.) from the fabric. Pull gently on the bobbin thread to pull a loop of the top thread down through the fabric. Slip a pin into this loop and pull the top thread right through, so that both ends of thread are on the wrong side of the fabric.

2 Tie a single knot, but take one end of the thread twice through the loop formed by the other end before tightening the knot. Tie a second knot in the usual way. This is called a surgeon's knot and the double twist at the start prevents the first knot slipping loose while you tie the second one. Trim the ends of the thread about 1cm (⅜ in.) from the knot.

3 If the knot is going to come under strain, sew in the ends of the threads. Thread the ends into a hand-sewing needle and either weave the needle in and out of a few stitches, or make tiny backstitches in the seam allowance, as shown. When weaving in and out of stitches, be careful to take the needle under them and not split the stitches with the tip of the needle.

1.

2.

3.

Above: a line of stitching secured by reversed stitches (top) and by knotted and sewn in threads (below).

Finishing edges

Most fabrics will fray to some degree, so the raw, cut edges of an open seam allowance need to be finished – or neatened as it's also called – to prevent them eventually fraying so far that the seam splits. The method of finishing you choose will depend on how much your fabric frays, how special the project is, whether the seam allowances are visible and whether they will be subject to wear and tear.

1.

2.

3.

4.

5.

6.

6a.

Check out...

Stitches, page 23

How to run a sewing machine, page 21

Pressing, pages 26-27

Sewing straight lines, page 30

Open seam, page 34

Zigzag bias binding, page 78

Best used for...

Open seams

All fabrics that fray

1 Items such as fancy dress costumes or cushions made from fabric that doesn't fray much, can just have their seam allowances trimmed with pinking shears. This is perfectly adequate for projects that don't need to last or won't get much wear, but not for anything else.

2 The most commonly used method of finishing seam allowances is zigzagging them. All but the most ancient of sewing machines will have a zigzag function. Test the width and tightness of the zigzag on a scrap of the project fabric and adjust it until it fits within the seam allowance and doesn't pucker the fabric. Press the seam open then zigzag stitch along each allowance in turn. Trim them afterwards if necessary.

3 If you are in a hurry and the project isn't special, then you can zigzag the allowances together. Press the seam open, then press it flat again. Set up the zigzag stitch as before, then zigzag stitch along both allowances together. Trim them if necessary, then press them to one side.

4 If your machine has an overcasting function, then you can use that to finish the allowances in a similar way to zigzagging.

5 For seams that will be visible, zigzag binding is practical and good-looking, though it is time consuming. If you can cut fabric and sew seams very accurately, then consider binding all the edges of the project pieces before sewing them together; it's easier, but hard to change if you get anything wrong. Otherwise, bind the seam allowances after sewing the seam. Turn to Zigzag Bias Binding (page 78) for instructions.

6 Pinked, open zigzagged, overcast and bound seams can be topstitched for added security, and the lines of stitching are a great finishing detail on the right side (see 6a.). This is practical for thick fabrics or fabrics that are difficult to press so the seam allowances don't lie very flat.

Finish the seam allowances using the desired method. Right side up, place the fabric under the machine with the edge of the presser foot against the seam. Keeping the edge of the foot against the seam so the stitching is beautifully straight, topstitch the length of the seam, sewing through the main fabric and seam allowance.

Repeat on the other side of the seam, starting from the same end as before. Working in the same direction on each side of the seam prevents the fabric distorting.

You can topstitch seam allowances that have been zigzagged together with a single line of topstitching on one side of the seam. However, this can make for a bulky seam, so experiment on a scrap of the fabric first.

Trimming and layering seams

If a seam is joining more than two layers of fabric, or if a fabric is very thick, the seam can become bulky. This can make it lie badly or show on the right side of the fabric when the seam is pressed. Trimming the seam allowances can cure these problems.

Check out...

Pressing, pages 26–27
Sewing straight lines, page 30
Finishing edges, page 32
Open seam, page 34

Best used for...

Open seams
All fabrics, especially
   heavyweight ones

Trimming

When two layers of thick fabric are seamed, carefully trim off up to two-thirds of one or both seam allowances using small scissors. Trimming one seam allowance only will mean that the two no longer align and so will produce less of a bump if they are pressed to the same side. Trimming both seam allowances makes the seam less bulky if it is being pressed open. If you are concerned about the fabric fraying, either trim with pinking shears or finish the edge after trimming it.

Above: seam allowances with one allowance trimmed and both zigzagged.

Layering

If there are several layers of fabric in a seam, then trim them to different depths. Above, the seam allowance of the main fabric (the striped fabric) has been left the full width. The interfacing has been trimmed to about 1cm (⅜ in.) and the lining to about 5mm (¼ in.). The edge of the main fabric could be finished by zigzagging or overcasting; the interfacing won't fray so it can be left as it is; and the lining is trimmed with pinking shears as it would be tricky to finish such a narrow seam allowance in any other way.

If the fabric is interfaced with sew-in interfacing, as above, then that can be trimmed very close to the line of stitching as it won't fray. If you are using iron-on interfacing, then trim it before ironing it onto the fabric and sewing the seam.

Shaped seams

These also need to be trimmed, but in slightly different ways depending on whether they are corners, curves or points. Turn to Around The Corner (pages 64–71) to find out how to deal with the seam allowances on these shapes.

Open seam

This is the most basic seam and the one that you will use most often. Although it's easy to do, it's worth learning to sew it smoothly and well, as all of your projects will look better when the seams are perfect.

Check out...

Stitches, page 23

How to run a sewing machine, page 21

Pinning, page 24

Tacking, page 25

Pressing, pages 26-27

Sewing straight lines, page 30

Starting and finishing sewing, page 31

Finishing edges, page 32

Best used for...

Straight seams

Gently curved seams

All fabrics, especially heavyweight ones

1 Right sides together, pin the two pieces to be seamed and, if necessary, tack them 1cm (⅜ in.) from the raw edges.

2 Set the sewing machine to a medium straight stitch. Position the fabric in the sewing machine to take a 1.5cm (⅝ in.) seam allowance. If the ends of the seam are going to be reversed to secure the stitching, position the fabric so that the needle will start sewing about 1cm (⅜ in.) from the start of the seam.

Left: an open seam on the right side of the project (above) and on the wrong side (below).

3 Sew in reverse for 1cm (⅜ in.), then machine-sew forwards to sew the seam. When you reach the other end, sew in reverse for 1cm (⅜ in.).

4 Remove the tacking stitches. Press the seamed area flat, then press the seam allowances open. Finish the edges of the seam allowances as desired.

Mock French seam

Easier to sew than a traditional French seam, a mock French seam completely encloses the raw edges of the fabric, giving a beautifully neat finish on the reverse. Don't use it for heavyweight fabrics as the result will be both bulky and stiff. This seam, the French Seam (page 36), and Self-bound Seam (page 37), all have a little ridge on the inside that's made by the enclosed seam allowances, so these seams are not great for tight-fitting garments.

Check out...

Stitches, page 23

How to run a sewing machine, page 21

Pinning, page 24

Tacking, page 25

Pressing, pages 26–27

Sewing straight lines, page 30

Starting and finishing sewing, page 31

Open seam, page 34

Best used for...

Straight seams

Gently curved seams

Sheer, lightweight and mediumweight fabrics

Seams where the reverse is visible

Seams where the reverse will be subject to wear and tear

1 Sew the pieces together following Steps 1–4 of Open Seam, but do not finish the seam allowances. Fold one of the pressed-open seam allowances in half so that the raw edge of the fabric just touches the line of stitching. Press the fold.

2 Fold in and press the other seam allowance in the same way.

3 Fold the fabric flat so that the right sides are together. Press the seamed area flat again, so that the folded edges of the seam allowances are touching.

4 Position the fabric in the sewing machine so that the needle will start sewing very close to the folded edges. You can check if the fabric is in the correct position by turning the handwheel to lower the needle until it just touches the fabric. Machine-sew the edges together, then knot the threads to secure them (it's quite tricky to reverse-stitch a seam so close to the edge).

5 Press the seamed area, then open the fabric out flat and press the enclosed seam allowance to one side.

Right: a mock French seam on the right side of the project (above) and on the wrong side (below).

French seam

This is a classic seam that encloses the raw edges of the fabric to create a neat finish on both sides of the work. It's particularly good for sheer fabrics, such as the cotton organdie that is being used here, but not for fabrics that fray very easily. You need to be careful and accurate when trimming the allowances in Step 2 so that no stray threads poke out through the final line of stitching.

Check out...

Stitches, page 23
How to run a sewing machine, page 21
Pinning, page 24
Tacking, page 25
Pressing, pages 26-27
Sewing straight lines, page 30
Starting and finishing sewing, page 31
Open seam, page 34

Best used for...

Straight seams
Sheer, lightweight and mediumweight fabrics
Seams where the reverse is visible
Seams where the reverse will be subject to wear and tear

1.

2.

3.

4.

5.

1 Pin the pieces of fabric together with the WRONG SIDES facing each other. Sew the pieces together following Steps 1–3 of Open Seam, but taking a 1cm (⅜ in.) seam allowance. Press the seamed area flat, but do not press the seam allowances open.

2 Trim both of the seam allowances to approximately 3mm (⅛ in.).

3 Along the seam, fold the fabric so that the RIGHT SIDES are facing each other and the trimmed seam is hidden in the fold. Pin the layers together.

4 Put the fabric under the foot of the machine with the folded edge 5mm (¼ in.) from the needle. Many machines do not have a 5mm (¼ in.) mark on the throat plate, so either measure out from the needle and mark the distance with masking tape, or use a 5mm (¼ in.) presser foot, as here. Sew the seam, reversing at each end to secure the stitching.

5 Press the seamed area, then open the fabric out flat and press the enclosed seam allowance to one side.

Left: a French seam on the right side of the project (above) and on the wrong side (below).

Self-bound seam

Of all the seams with enclosed edges this is the best one for fabrics that fray easily, such as the dupion silk used here, but don't use it for heavyweight fabrics. The reverse is not quite as attractive as that of the Mock French Seam (page 35) and French Seam (opposite), but it will be durable.

1.

2.

3.

4.

5.

Check out...
Stitches, page 23
How to run a sewing machine, page 21
Pinning, page 24
Tacking, page 25
Pressing, pages 26–27
Sewing straight lines, page 30
Starting and finishing sewing, page 31
Open seam, page 34

Best used for...
Straight seams
Lightweight and mediumweight fabrics
Fabrics that fray easily
Seams where the reverse will be subject to wear and tear

1 Sew the pieces together following Steps 1–4 of Open Seam, but do not finish the seam allowances. Trim one of the seam allowances to 5mm (¼ in.).

2 Press the trimmed allowance over so that it lies flat on top of the untrimmed allowance.

3 Fold over the edge of the untrimmed allowance until it almost, but not quite, touches the trimmed edge. Press the fold.

4 Fold the pressed edge over the trimmed edge so that the pressed fold lies along the line of stitching of the original seam. The fold shouldn't overlap the stitching or the seam can look lumpy on the right side.

5 Fold the fabric right sides together along the original seam and press the folded seam allowances. Position the fabric in the sewing machine so that the needle will start sewing very close to the folded edge: you can check this by turning the handwheel to lower the needle until it just touches the fabric. Machine-sew the seam. Press the seamed area, then open the fabric out flat and press the enclosed seam allowance to one side so that the folded-over edge is uppermost.

Right: a self-bound seam on the right side of the project (above) and on the wrong side (below).

Flat fell seam

Probably best known as the type of seam that runs down the outside leg of a pair of jeans, the flat fell seam is robust, suitable for heavyweight fabrics and, unlike all the other enclosed seams, it is flat on the reverse and so very comfortable to wear. It does require a beautifully straight line of stitching to finish it in Step 5.

Check out...

Stitches, page 23

How to run a sewing machine, page 21

Pinning, page 24

Tacking, page 25

Pressing, pages 26–27

Sewing straight lines, page 30

Starting and finishing sewing, page 31

Open seam, page 34

Best used for...

Straight seams

Mediumweight and heavyweight fabrics

Seams where the reverse will be subject to wear and tear

1 Pin the pieces of fabric together with the WRONG SIDES facing each other. Sew the pieces together following Steps 1–4 of Open Seam, but do not finish the seam allowances. Trim one of the seam allowances to 5mm (¼ in.).

2 Press the trimmed allowance over so that it lies flat on top of the untrimmed allowance.

3 Fold over the edge of the untrimmed allowance so that it touches the trimmed edge. Press the fold.

4 Press the whole of the untrimmed allowance over so that it covers the trimmed one and all the raw edges are hidden.

5 Position the fabric in the sewing machine so that the needle will start sewing very close to the folded edge. You can check that the fabric is in the right position by turning the handwheel to lower the needle until it just touches the fabric. Machine-sew very close to the

folded edge to complete the seam. Press the seam flat.

Left: a flat fell seam on the right side of the project (above) and on the wrong side (below).

Intersecting seams

Seams that cross or meet need to be treated in a particular way to avoid lumps of stacked seam allowances. This sample shows seams crossing one another, but the same principles apply if two seams form a T-shape.

Right: intersecting seams on the right side of the project (above) and on the wrong side (below).

1 Sew the first pieces together following Steps 1–3 of Open Seam. Press the seamed area flat, but do not press the seam allowances open. At the end of the seam that will intersect, trim the seam allowances to a point, starting to cut about 2cm (¾ in.) from the end of the seam and sloping the cut to end about 3mm (⅛ in.) from the line of stitching. Trimming the seam allowance with pinking shears will help prevent fraying without adding bulk.

2 Press the seam allowances open. Repeat Steps 1–2 on the other intersecting piece.

3 Measuring accurately, press under the seam allowance (across the trimmed end of the first seam) on one of the pieces to be joined.

4 Lay the pressed piece on the other piece, 1.5cm (⅝ in.) from the raw edge and match up the seams perfectly. Pin the pieces together, then press the top seam allowance flat again.

5 Taking a 1.5cm (⅝ in.) seam allowance, sew the new seam as for an Open Seam. Stitch carefully over the ends of the first seams, being sure not to ruck up or pucker the seam allowances.

6 Press the new seam flat, then press it open.

Check out...
Stitches, page 23
How to run a sewing machine, page 21
Pinning, page 24
Tacking, page 25
Pressing, pages 26–27
Sewing straight lines, page 30

Starting and finishing sewing, page 31
Open seam, page 34

Best used for...
Lightweight and mediumweight fabrics

Hemmed in

Many of your sewing projects will need a hem somewhere, whether it's the lower edge of a skirt, the top edge of a bag or the opening of a pillowcase. A smooth, beautifully stitched hem of the right type for the project will help give your work that finish that carries it over the line from homemade into handmade.

Hem allowance

The amount of fabric folded over to make the hem is called the hem allowance. On lightweight fabrics this is usually 2.5cm (1 in.) for a single hem and for a double hem – the most commonly used type – it will usually be 3.5cm (1⅜ in.). Always check a pattern to see what it specifies.

Hem allowances on heavier fabrics can be up to 8cm (3 in.), as narrow hems on thick fabrics become stiff and bulky. Curtains will routinely have a hem allowance of up to 20cm (8 in.).

You can add extra to the hem allowance on children's garments to allow for letting the hem down as they grow, but bear in mind that too deep a hem will hang oddly. When the hem is let down there may be a permanent mark on the fabric along the original fold line. This mark can be disguised by sewing ribbon or braid over it (see Sewing On Ribbon Or Braid, page 90), but a fashion-conscious child may not be thrilled by this idea.

Single hem

Above: a single hem on the right side of the project (left) and on the wrong side (right).

This is the most basic of hems and is only suitable if either the edge being turned up is the selvedge or if the project doesn't need to wear well – a Halloween outfit maybe – and the raw edge can be zigzagged. Selvedges are tempting to use, but can cause problems so read the box below before using such an edge.

Check out...

Stitches, page 23

How to run a sewing machine, page 21

Pinning, page 24

Pressing, pages 26–27

Starting and finishing sewing, page 31

Best used for...

Straight hems

Selvedge edges

All fabrics

1 Using a ruler or seam gauge to check the measurement right along the hem, fold the selvedge edge of the fabric over by 2.5cm (1 in.). Press the fold.

2 Pin the selvedge edge in place. Set the sewing machine to a medium straight stitch. Put the fabric under the presser foot of the machine with the edge of the foot against the selvedge edge. Machine-sew the hem, removing pins as you get to them and reversing at each end to secure the stitching.

Selvedges

The selvedge is the edge along the length of the fabric: it is created during production of the fabric and won't fray. Woven fabrics, such as the one used here, usually have a selvedge that is the same colour as the main part of the fabric, but it can have a slightly different, tighter weave. This can shrink during washing, which would make a selvedge-edge hem pucker unattractively and permanently. Printed fabrics usually have a white selvedge – often with the manufacturer's name printed on it – and that, too, can be of a different weave. If you want to use a selvedge, wash a bit of the fabric first to see what happens.

Double hem

The most commonly used type of hem, this gives a neat finish by enclosing the raw edge. If the fabric frays readily, then either trim the raw edge with pinking shears or zigzag it before making the first fold.

Above: a double hem on the right side of the project (left) and on the wrong side (right).

Check out...

1 Using a ruler or seam gauge to check the measurement right along the hem, fold the edge of the fabric over by 1cm (⅜ in.). Press the fold.

2 Fold the fabric over by a further 2.5cm (1 in.) and press this second fold. Pin the folded edge in place and machine-sew the hem as for a Single Hem, positioning the edge of the foot against the first pressed fold.

Best used for...

Straight hems
All fabrics

Narrow hem

It can be difficult to make a very narrow double hem, especially on sheer fabrics. This method is quick, easy and successful. You need a hem allowance the desired width of the double hem, plus 1.5cm (⅝ in.).

Check out...

Best used for...

Straight hems
Sheer and lightweight fabrics

1 Using a ruler or seam gauge to check the measurement right along the hem, fold the edge of the fabric over by 1.5cm (⅝ in.) and pin in place. Set the sewing machine to a medium straight stitch and machine-sew along the folded edge, sewing very close to the fold.

2 Trim the seam allowance close to the line of stitching. The distance between the folded edge and the trimmed edge establishes the depth of the hem.

3 Fold the hem over to enclose the raw edge and machine-sew again, sewing over the first line of stitching to complete the hem.

Below: a narrow hem on the right side of the project (left) and on the wrong side (right).

Blind-stitch hem

Above: a blind-stitch hem on the right side of the project (left) and on the wrong side (right).

This is a hem that relies on your sewing machine having a blind-stitch setting, but it is a fairly basic function and most modern machines will have it. It can require a bit of fiddling about to get a perfect result, so check the instruction manual for your sewing machine for any specific information and practise on a spare piece of the fabric first before hemming a project.

Check out...

Best used for...

Straight hems
All fabrics

1.

2.

1 Follow Steps 1–2 of Double Hem.

2 Fold the pressed hem to the right side of the main fabric so that just a small amount of the 1 cm (⅜ in.) hem is visible, as shown. The precise amount that needs to be visible will depend on the settings your sewing machine uses, so this is where the manual and practice come in.

3 Set the sewing machine to the blind-stitch setting and fit the correct presser foot (this will usually be a zigzag foot or a special blind-hem foot). Turn the handwheel until the needle is at the furthest right position and then put the fabric in the machine so that the needle goes into the visible section of the folded-under hem.

4 As you sew the hem, the needle will move across to the left and at its furthest left position it should be going down into the fabric just over the folded-back edge. The needle should not be right on the fold or the stitch will not catch enough of the fabric to make the hem secure. It also should not be too far over the fold or the stitch will be very visible on the right side. Experiment on your spare piece of fabric until you've got the position of the fabric under the needle exactly right, then, if necessary, mark the position of the right-hand edge of the fabric on the throat plate with a piece of masking tape.

3.

4.

Curved hem

Above: a curved hem on the right side of the project (left) and on the wrong side (right).

Projects with curved edges – such as a circular skirt or a round tablecloth – will need this hemming technique. The tacking might seem a little time-consuming, but it is worth doing for a perfect finish. Remember to test the fabric marker on a scrap of the fabric to make sure the mark will disappear.

1 Using a ruler or seam gauge to measure accurately, mark concentric lines 3.5cm (1⅜ in.) and 1cm (⅜ in.) in from the edge of the fabric. The best way to do this is to make a line of marks 5cm (2 in.) apart, then join them freehand.

2 Using a contrast-coloured thread, tack along both marked lines. You can use quite long tacking stitches, but try to make them fairly even in length. Leave long tails of thread at each end of the tacked line nearest the raw edge.

3 Fold the fabric over along this lower tacked line and press the fold. Don't worry about pressing any puckers or gathers in the folded-over fabric, just concentrate on getting a smooth hem line.

4 Fold the fabric over along the upper tacked line, but do not press the fold at this stage. Put in lots of vertical pins – heads facing out – to hold the hem in position. Again, don't worry about puckers in the fabric, concentrate on making the hem line a smooth curve.

5 Gently pull on the long tails of thread left at each end of the lower tacked line. Working methodically along the hem, pull up and adjust the gathers evenly until the inner edge lies as flat as possible.

6 Tack along the inner edge of the hem, using small stitches to tack the gathers in place. Press the hem, pressing the gathers flat.

7 Set the sewing machine to a medium straight stitch. Put the fabric under the machine with the edge of the foot against the inner hem line. Machine-sew the hem, sewing carefully over the gathers to prevent them pushing up into lumpy groups. Remove the tacking stitches and press the finished hem thoroughly.

Check out...

Best used for...

All fabrics

Corner hem

The idea of having to produce a square, flat, mitred corner is one that sends many novice sewers pale, but it isn't a difficult technique to get right, you just need to be able to measure and press accurately. As usual, the raw edges can be overcast or zigzagged if you are worried about the fabric fraying.

Best used for...

All fabrics

1.

2.

3.

1 Using a ruler or seam gauge to measure accurately, fold the edges of the fabric over by 1 cm (⅜ in.) and press the folds. Fold the edges over by another 2.5cm (1 in.) and press these second folds.

2 Open the pressed hems out flat and lay the fabric right side down. At the corner, fold over a triangle of fabric: the point where the second pressed lines cross should be in the middle of the folded-over edge. Press the corner fold flat.

3 Open the corner out then, right sides together, fold the corner in half, matching the raw edges and the ends of the pressed corner fold. Pin the layers together along the pressed corner fold, with the head of the pin facing towards the raw edges of the fabric.

Left: a corner hem on the right side of the project. Right: and on the wrong side.

4 Set the sewing machine to a medium straight stitch. Starting at the fold, machine-sew along the pressed corner line as far as the first pressed hem line, reversing at each end to secure the stitching.

5 Trim off the corner of fabric 5mm (¼ in.) above the line of stitching. At the folded edge, clip off a little more fabric at an angle, as shown.

6 Open the corner out square along the second pressed hem lines. Press the edge trimmed in Step 5 to one side. The clipped angle – which is now at the point – should sit neatly inside the square corner.

7 Turn the corner right side out and re-press the second hem lines so that everything lies square and flat.

8 Turn under the first pressed hem lines and pin them in place.

9 Put the fabric under the machine with the edge of the foot against the first hem line. Machine-sew the hem, pivoting the fabric around the needle at the square corner. Press the hemmed edges and corner thoroughly.

Taped hem

Above: a slip-stitched taped hem on the right side of the project (left) and on the wrong side (right).

If you don't have enough fabric for a double hem (maybe because you are letting a garment down), then a taped hem is a great solution. It's also good for very heavy fabrics where a double hem would be very bulky. This example uses a lightweight fabric and ribbon, but for heavyweight fabrics you should use purpose-made hem tape. Before sewing on the ribbon, zigzag the raw edge of the fabric if it frays easily.

Check out...

Best used for...

Straight hems
All fabrics, particularly
   heavyweight ones

1.

2.

3.

4.

1 Using a ruler or seam gauge to check the measurement along the hem, fold the edge of the fabric over by 1cm (⅜ in.). Press the fold.

2 Lay the fabric flat and pin the ribbon to the right side, 5mm (¼ in.) below the fold.

3 Set the sewing machine to a medium straight stitch. Put the fabric under the presser foot of the machine with the edge of the foot against the pressed fold: when you start sewing the line of stitching should be on the ribbon, very close to the upper edge. Machine-sew the ribbon to the fabric.

4 Re-fold the fabric along the line pressed in Step 1, then you have a choice of finishing technique. You can machine-sew along the other edge of the ribbon or you can slip stitch it by hand, as shown. Slip stitching is almost invisible on the right side, but if you machine-sew the edge then the line of stitching will be visible (see Step 6, Faced Hem, opposite).

Choosing ribbon or tape

The ribbon or tape must be a similar weight to the fabric, so don't use lightweight ribbon on thick woollen fabric. Also, you must take laundering into account: the ribbon and the fabric must be wash-compatible. Once you've resolved these practical issues, consider the look of the thing. A pretty, patterned tape will be seen by almost no-one except you, but you'll know it's there. It adds a fabulous finishing touch and those who do catch a glimpse will be impressed.

Faced hem

This style of hem is similar to the Taped Hem and is great if you are short of your main fabric, but as you are joining two fabrics close to the hem line it's not good for heavyweight fabrics because the seam will create bulk. Again, it's a perfect opportunity to add a designerly touch to a project by facing the hem in a fabric that complements – or contrasts with – the main fabric. The facing should be between 7cm (2¾ in.) and 4cm (1½ in.) deep and should be of a fabric that is a similar weight and fibre content as the main fabric. The technique is shown here on a straight hem, but you can also use it on curved hems, just cut the facing to match the curve of the main fabric.

1. Cut a facing the required depth plus 3cm (1¼ in.) for hem and seam allowances. Turn under and press a 1.5cm (⅝ in.) hem along the upper edge of the facing. Right sides together and matching the raw edges, pin the facing to the main fabric.

2. Set the sewing machine to a medium straight stitch. Using thread to match the facing and taking a 1.5cm (⅝ in.) seam allowance, machine-sew the facing to the hem.

3. Trim the seam allowance of the main fabric to about half its depth. This edge can be cut with pinking shears if the fabric has a tendency to fray.

4. Press the seam flat then press the facing flat, pressing both seam allowances towards the facing.

5. Understitch the facing by sewing a line of machine stitching 3mm (⅛ in.) from the seamline, sewing through both seam allowances and the facing.

6. Fold the facing to the wrong side of the main fabric, folding over just a tiny amount of the main fabric at the same time to ensure that none of the facing shows on the right side. Press the fold. You can finish the top edge as for a Taped Hem by either slip stitching or machine-sewing it. If you slip stitch then choose a thread colour to match the main fabric. If you machine-sew, then sew with the facing uppermost and match the spool thread to the facing and the bobbin thread to the main fabric for best results.

Check out...

Best used for...
Straight and curved hems
Lightweight and mediumweight fabrics

Fastened up

Zips, buttonholes, ties and rouleaux loops are all fastenings you'll want to use in your sewing projects. There are tips and tricks for inserting and making them that will make the tasks easier and the end results look better.

Centred zip

This style of zip is typically used to fasten a skirt or trousers. Zips can seem daunting, but if you follow these instructions carefully you'll find it easy to insert one. The technique is exactly the same for the different types of zip – concealed zip, dress zip or metal-toothed zip.

Best used for...

Zip that opens at the top of a seam

1 Mark with a pin the position in the seam where the end of the zip will be. Sew the seam up to the pin, take the pin out and reverse a few stitches to secure the end of the seam.

2 Using a fabric marker, mark the seamline on the open section of the seam, where the zip will be. Tack along the marked seamline, using short, tight tacking stitches to close the open section of the seam.

3 Press the whole seam – the machine-sewn section and the tacked section – open. At this stage you should finish the edges of the seam allowances by either zigzagging or overcasting them.

4 With the fabric right side down, position the end stop of the zip on the machine-sewn section of the

seam, just below the start of the tacking. Align the teeth with the seamline and pin the zip in place through the tape. Lay the zip along the tacked section of the seam, keeping the teeth aligned with the seamline and pinning it in place.

5 Tack the zip in position, tacking through the zip tape on both sides of the teeth. Tack in the middle of the tape to avoid the stitches getting entangled in the machine-sewing.

6 When you are machine-sewing the zip, you'll need to move the pull and on some zips this is easier to do by pulling up than by pushing down. Test yours to see how easily the pull moves in each direction and if it is trickier to push down, then wriggle it down to the halfway point now, before you start sewing.

7 Set the sewing machine to a medium straight stitch and fit the zip foot. Position the top of the zip under the foot with the side of the foot against the zip teeth, so that the needle will start sewing as close to the teeth as possible. Sewing quite slowly, sew the zip in place – keeping the edge of the zip foot running along the teeth of the zip – until just before you reach the pull.

8 Stop sewing with the needle down in the fabric. Lift the presser foot and wriggle the pull past the needle. This can be a bit tricky and you may need to pivot the fabric around the needle, which is fine as long as the needle remains firmly in place in the fabric. Don't move the pull up to the top, just enough to get it past the needle. Straighten the fabric, lower the presser foot and continue sewing to the bottom of the zip, just below the end stop.

9 Sew across the zip tape below the end stop. Cut and knot the threads to secure the stitching.

10 Move the zip foot to the other side. Starting at the top of the zip, repeat Steps 7–8 to sew the other side of the zip tape in place, knotting the threads at the bottom to secure the stitching. Sewing from the top down on both sides of the zip prevents the fabric twisting.

11 Using sharp embroidery scissors and the tip of a darning needle, cut and pull the tacking stitches out of the seam. Press the fabric flat over the zip.

Zip trick

If you are making a skirt or trousers with a waistband and a centred or lapped zip, then buy a zip that is about 5cm (2 in.) longer than you need. Prepare the seam and position the zip end stop as usual. Pin the zip in place so that the top, and the pull, protrude above the edge of the fabric. Sew the zip in place quickly and easily, without having to wriggle the pull past the needle. Unpick the tacking, open the zip, cut the protruding top section off and sew the waistband over the teeth at the top of the zip. So simple and clever.

Above: a centred zip.

Inset zip

You'll use this zip in the middle of a seam, perhaps in the side seam of a dress or across the back of a large cushion. The principle is very similar to a centred zip.

Best used for...

Zip that opens in the middle of a seam

1 Follow Steps 1–2 of Centred Zip, putting in a pin to mark both ends of the zip and sewing both ends of the seam. Tack the open centre section.

2 Press the whole seam – the machine-sewn section and the tacked section – open. At this stage you should finish the edges of the seam allowances by either zigzagging or overcasting them.

3 Follow Steps 4–6 of Centred Zip to pin then tack the zip in position.

4 At the top of the zip, tack the toothless section of the tape together above the zip pull.

5 Follow Steps 7–11 of Centred Zip to machine-sew the zip in place and finish it. Machine-sew across the tacked tape at the top, down one side and across the end. Then sew down the other side, starting from the top.

Left: an inset zip.

Separating zip

This is the type of zip typically used on a jacket; the two halves separate completely at the bottom. Nylon zips of this style are usually available in just a narrow range of colours, with the metal-toothed ones being more easily found.

Best used for...

Zip that needs to
   open completely

1 Finish the edges of the fabric before you insert the zip. Separate the zip and lay the side with the pull right side down on the right side of one piece of fabric. Match the edge of the zip tape with the raw edge of the fabric. Pin then tack this side of the zip in position.

2 Follow Steps 7–8 of Centred Zip to machine-sew the zip in place. Knot the threads at the back at each end.

3 Fold the zip tape to the wrong side of the fabric, so that only the teeth show on the right side. Press the fold.

4 Zip the free side of the zip onto the sewn-on side.

5 With the zip flat and right side up, lay the other piece of fabric right side down on top of it. Match the raw edge of the fabric with the edge of the zip tape and pin then tack them together.

6 Separate the zip again. Machine-sew, then fold and press the second side of the zip in place in the same way as for the first side. Remove all tacking stitches.

Right: a separating zip. You can topstitch the fabric close to the zip teeth to help hold the zip tape flat; the left-hand side of this sample has been topstitched.

Lapped zip

As with a centred zip, this style is used for skirts and trousers, but it's more professional-looking as a flap of fabric completely covers the zip teeth. There are some complicated ways of inserting this style of zip, but this method is straightforward. You may find that you prefer it – as I do – to a centred zip for looks and ease of insertion. In this example the overlap is on the right-hand side, so the zip would be on the left-hand side of the body.

Check out...
Stitches, page 23
How to run a sewing machine, page 21
Pinning, page 24
Tacking, page 25
Pressing, pages 26-27
Sewing straight lines, page 30
Starting and finishing sewing, page 31
Finishing edges, page 32
Open seam, page 34
Centred zip, pages 52-53

Best used for...
Zip that opens at the top of a seam

1 Follow Step I of Centred Zip to sew the seam below where the zip will be. Using a seam gauge to measure accurately, press the 1.5cm (⅝ in.) allowances on the open section of the seam to the wrong side. Finish the seam allowances by zigzagging or overcasting them.

2 Lay the fabric right side up with the open end of the seam towards you. Open the left-hand seam allowance out and then re-press 1cm (⅜ in.) to the wrong side. On the right side you'll see the original pressed line then a further 5mm (¼ in.) of fabric.

Right: a lapped zip.

3 Lay one side of the zip under the edge of the left-hand piece of fabric, positioning it so that the folded edge is against the zip teeth. Pin then tack it in place, tacking along the line pressed in Step 1, the edge of the original seam allowance.

4 Set the sewing machine to a medium straight stitch and fit the zip foot. Right side up, position the top of the zip under the foot with the side of the foot against the zip teeth, so that the needle will start sewing as close to the teeth as possible. Have the right-hand piece of fabric folded right side down across the side you are sewing. Machine-sew the tacked side of the zip in place.

5 As you get towards the bottom of the zip, make sure the right-hand piece of fabric is completely out of the way so that you can sew past the start of the seam to sew the tape to the seam allowance right down to the bottom of the zip.

6.

7.

8.

9.

6 With the fabric right side up, lay the right-hand piece over the zip, matching the folded edge with the line on the left-hand side that was pressed in Step 1. Pin the flap in place.

7 Turn the fabric over. On the wrong side, tack the free side of the zip tape to the fabric. Keep the stitches in a straight line, as they will be your guide when it comes to machine-sewing this side of the zip.

8 Right side up, position the fabric under the foot so that the needle will start sewing along the line of tacking stitches worked in Step 7. This is one occasion where you will be sewing over tacking stitches and you'll need to pick them out afterward. Machine-sew from the top to the bottom of the zip.

9 With the needle down in the fabric, lift the presser foot and pivot the fabric 90° around the needle. Sew across the bottom of the flap. Knot the threads on the back to secure the stitching. Remove all tacking stitches.

Shortening a zip

Sometimes you won't be able to get a zip that's the right length, but for centred, inset and lapped zips it's very easy to shorten a longer one as needed. This technique works on all nylon-toothed zips; for metal-toothed ones, follow Step 1, then use craft pliers to pull off a couple of the zip teeth 1 cm (⅜ in.) below the stitches so that you can cut the tape without damaging your shears.

Check out...

Centred zip, pages 52–53
Inset zip, page 54
Lapped zip, pages 56–57

Best used for...

Centred, inset and lapped zips

1 Thread a needle with doubled sewing thread in a colour that matches the zip (a contrast colour is used here for clarity). At the required length, make five or six firm, straight stitches over the zip teeth. Secure the thread with a couple of backstitches in the zip tape.

2 Using pinking shears, cut off the zip about 1 cm (⅜ in.) below the stitches.

1.

2.

Automatic buttonhole

This function is not found on all machines, but is one that I recommend. It makes professional-looking buttonholes quickly and easily. Different sewing machines may have slightly different ways of making automatic buttonholes, so read your manual before trying one.

Check out...

Buying your first sewing
    machine, page 13
Stitches, page 23
How to run a sewing machine,
    page 21
Pressing, pages 26-27

Best used for...

Buttonholes in fabric

1 Fit the button you want to use into the buttonhole foot. The machine will automatically make a buttonhole the right size.

2 Mark the position of the buttonhole on the fabric.

3 Position the fabric under the foot so that the needle will start sewing at the end of the buttonhole nearest to you. Set the machine to the buttonhole function. Gently press the power pedal and the machine will sew the buttonhole. You need to be prepared to do some gentle steering, particularly when making buttonholes near seams, as lumps or ridges in the fabric can throw the buttonhole off

course. When the buttonhole is complete, pull the threads through to the back and trim them off.

4 Press the stitching. Put a pin in at each end of the buttonhole, just inside the end bars. These will make sure that you don't cut the threads by accident.

5 Using small, sharp-pointed scissors, very carefully cut the buttonhole open. Push one point of the scissors into the fabric in the middle of the buttonhole to start cutting to one end, then turn around and cut to the other end.

Manual buttonhole

If you don't have an automatic buttonhole function on your machine, then you can make buttonholes manually, but do practise first as they are tricky to get right. On some machines the zigzag is not as tight stitched in reverse as it is stitched forwards, so the two sides of the buttonhole won't match perfectly.

Check out...
Stitches, page 23
How to run a sewing machine, page 21
Pressing, pages 26–27
Automatic buttonhole, page 58

Best used for...
Buttonholes in fabric

1 Mark the position of the buttonhole on the fabric. Set the sewing machine to a wide zigzag with zero stitch length. Position the fabric under the foot so that the needle will start sewing at the end of the buttonhole nearest to you. Make four or five stitches, ending with the needle on the left-hand side, but not down in the fabric.

2 Set the machine to a very narrow, tight zigzag. Press the reverse lever and slowly sew backwards along the length of the marked line. The right-hand edge of the stitching should just cover the line. End with the needle on the left-hand side, but not down in the fabric.

3 Reset the sewing machine to a wide zigzag with zero stitch length. Make four or five stitches, ending with the needle on the right-hand side, but not down in the fabric.

4 Reset the sewing machine to a very narrow, tight zigzag. Sew forwards until you reach the bar stitched in Step 1. The left-hand edge of the stitching should be very close to the stitches made in Step 2.

5 Pull all the threads through to the back. Thread them into a hand-sewing needle and weave them in and out of a few of the buttonhole stitches to secure them. Follow Steps 4–5 of Automatic Buttonhole to cut open the buttonhole.

Right: two automatic buttonholes (above), one with a button, and two manual buttonholes (below), one with a button.

In-seam buttonhole

This is essentially a gap in a seam through which you put a button and it is ridiculously simple to make. The pieces of thin fabric for the stays need to have the same laundering requirements as the main fabric.

Check out...

Stitches, page 23

How to run a sewing machine,
    page 21

Pinning, page 24

Pressing, pages 26–27

Sewing straight lines, page 30

Starting and finishing sewing,
    page 31

Finishing edges, page 32

Open seam, page 34

Best used for...

Buttonholes in seams

Above: two in-seam buttonholes, one with a button.

1 Using pinking shears, cut two pieces of very thin fabric (I have used organza – organdie or cotton lawn would also work), each 3cm (1¼ in.) wide by the required length of the buttonhole plus 2cm (¾ in.): these are the stays. Mark the length of the buttonhole centrally on one stay. On the main fabric, mark the seamline along the section where the buttonhole will be.

2 Lay the marked stay on the seamline where the buttonhole will be. Lay the other stay on the other side of the seam, matching the edges of them as best you can (they don't need to be perfectly aligned). Pin the stays in place, putting the pins in as you would if you were going to sew over them (which you aren't).

3 Set the sewing machine to a medium straight stitch and sew the seam up to the first pin. Reverse a few stitches to secure the seam. Turn the fabric around and sew the rest of the seam from the other end up to the other pin, reversing as before.

4 Press the seam open, then finish the edges of the seam allowances.

Ties

This technique can be used to make straps of any width and length to serve as bag handles, belts, dress straps and curtain tab tops, as well as ties.

Check out...

Stitches, page 23

How to run a sewing machine, page 21

Pinning, page 24

Pressing, pages 26–27

Sewing straight lines, page 30

Starting and finishing sewing, page 31

Outward square corner, page 67

Best used for...

Straps of any width and length

1 Cut on the straight grain a strip of fabric measuring four times the required width of the tie by the length plus 2cm (¾ in.). At each short end, press under 1cm (⅜ in.). Using small, sharp scissors, cut off the corners of the pressed-under section, as shown.

2 Wrong sides together, fold the tie in half along its length and press the fold.

3 Open the tie out flat. Fold one raw edge to the middle and press the fold along the length of the tie.

4 Fold in and press the other raw edge. Fold the whole tie in half along the line pressed in Step 2 and press it thoroughly.

5 Set the sewing machine to a medium straight stitch and fit the zip foot. At one end of the tie, position the fabric with the edge of the foot against the open edge of the tie, so that the needle will start sewing close to the edge. You can check that it is positioned correctly by turning the handwheel to lower the needle until it just touches the fabric. Topstitch along the edge, reversing at each end to secure the stitching. If the ends of the tie are going to be hidden in a seam, then there is no need to sew across them. If they are going to be on display, then start at the fold edge on one short end, sew across to very close to the open edge, put the needle down into the fabric and pivot the tie around it before topstitching the open edge. Repeat to topstitch the other short end of the tie.

Right: a tie.

Rouleaux loops

These pretty fastenings are often used on wedding dresses and evening gowns, though they work well on any project requiring a feminine touch. Each loop must be long enough for the button to pass through plus 3cm (1¼ in.), so experiment before cutting the loop lengths. The loops are sewn into a seam between the main fabric and a facing and it's usually best to use iron-on interfacing to stiffen the facing.

Check out...

Stitches, page 23

How to run a sewing machine, page 21

Pinning, page 24

Tacking, page 25

Pressing, pages 26–27

Sewing straight lines, page 30

Starting and finishing sewing, page 31

Finishing edges, page 32

Open seam, page 34

Making bias strip and binding, pages 74–75

Best used for...

Delicate fastenings

Lightweight and mediumweight fabrics

1 Cut a 2-cm (¾-in.) wide piece of bias fabric long enough to make the required number of loops. Right sides together, fold it in half along its length. Set the sewing machine to a medium straight stitch and fit a 5mm (¼ in.) patchwork foot. At one end of the strip, position the fabric with the edge of the foot against the open edge of the strip and sew the seam. Cut the threads leaving 15cm (6 in.) tails.

2 Thread a blunt-tipped darning needle with one of the tails of thread. Slide the needle up the tube of fabric, working it along until it appears at the other end.

3 Pull the thread through, coaxing the end of the fabric it's attached to turn in and emerge at the other end of the tube. Keep pulling gently (you really don't want the thread to snap) to turn the whole tube right side out.

4 Cut off pieces of tube the required length. Fold them in half and press them flat so that the folded ends look like this.

5 Pin each loop in position on the right side of the fabric, matching the ends of the loop with the raw edge of the fabric. Tack the loops in place.

10 Position the fabric under the needle with the presser foot on the seam allowances and the edge of it against the line of stitching. Understitch the facing by sewing the seam allowances to it.

11 Wrong sides together, fold the fabric and facing along the seam so that the loops protrude. Press the folded seam.

6 Fit a straight presser foot. Position the fabric under the needle with the edge of the presser foot against the raw edge of the fabric and machine-sew over the ends of each loop. Make sure that the loops remain at right angles to the raw edge of the fabric.

7 Right sides together, lay the facing on the main fabric, matching the raw edges. Pin the layers together and tack them if necessary.

8 Taking a 1.5cm (⅝ in.) seam allowance, machine-sew the facing to the main fabric. Remove all tacking stitches.

9 Press both the seam allowances towards the facing.

Right: rouleaux loops, two with buttons and two without.

Around the corner

Turning corners and sewing smooth curves are useful skills for all sorts of projects, from shirts to sheets. Done well, these techniques will lend a professional finish to your sewing and they aren't difficult to master.

Inward square corner

The place you'll see this corner most often is on a square neckline where the facing is sewn to the main fabric. The corner needs to be really flat and smooth for the neckline to lie properly. The same principle can also be used to sew more tightly or widely angled corners.

Check out...

Stitches, page 23

How to run a sewing machine,
  page 21

Pinning, page 24

Pressing, pages 26-27

Sewing straight lines, page 30

Starting and finishing sewing,
  page 31

Best used for...

Lightweight and
  mediumweight fabrics

1 On the first side you will sew, mark the end of the seam, 1.5cm (⅝ in.) beyond the corner. Pin the layers of fabric together.

2 Set the sewing machine to a medium straight stitch. Machine-sew the first side of the corner, stopping at the marked line with the needle down in the fabric.

3 Lift the presser foot and pivot the fabric around the needle until it is in the right position to sew the second side.

4 Machine-sew the second side of the corner.

5 Carefully snip into the seam allowances at the corner. Use the points of small scissors to snip down to about 3mm (⅛ in.) from the stitching.

6 Turn the corner right side out. Gently ease it into shape and press it thoroughly.

Left: an inward square corner.

Outward square corner

The corners of cushions and bags use this technique. Again, the same principle can also be used to sew more tightly or widely angled corners, though sharp points require a different treatment (see page 70).

1.

2.

3.

4.

Check out...

Stitches, page 23

How to run a sewing machine, page 21

Pinning, page 24

Pressing, pages 26–27

Sewing straight lines, page 30

Starting and finishing sewing, page 31

Inward square corner, page 66

Best used for...

Lightweight and mediumweight fabrics

Turning out corners

When you're turning the fabric right side out, do resist the temptation to use a knitting needle to push out the corner. It's all too easy to push the needle through the fabric or distort the corner beyond saving. Instead, use the end of a ruler, ideally a wooden or plastic one.

1 On the first side you will sew, mark the end of the seam, 1.5cm (⅝ in.) up from the edge. Pin the layers of fabric together.

2 Set the sewing machine to a medium straight stitch. Machine-sew the first seam, then lift the presser foot and pivot the fabric as for Step 3 of Inward Square Corner. Machine-sew the second side of the corner.

3 Cut off the seam allowance on one side of the corner. Start about 5cm (2 in.) from the corner and cut at an angle to within about 3mm (⅛ in.) of the stitching.

4 Cut off the seam allowance on the other side of the corner in the same way. Turn the corner right side out. Gently ease it into shape and press it thoroughly.

Right: an outward square corner.

Inward curve

Curved seams appear in many projects and it's worth learning how to treat the different curves to make them look their best. Inward curves require the seam allowances to be clipped so that they can stretch out to lie flat inside the curve.

Check out...

Stitches, page 23

How to run a sewing machine, page 21

Pinning, page 24

Pressing, pages 26–27

Sewing straight lines, page 30

Starting and finishing sewing, page 31

Open seam, page 34

Best used for...

All fabrics

1 Pin the layers of fabric together. Set the sewing machine to a medium straight stitch and machine-sew the seam, taking a 1.5cm (⅝ in.) seam allowance.

2 Trim the seam allowances to about half their original width.

3 Cutting at an angle, snip into one seam allowance, snipping down to about 3mm (⅛ in.) from the stitching. Make these snips all the way along the curve, spacing them evenly about 2cm (¾ in.) apart.

4 Snip into the other seam allowance in the same way. Make the snips at the same angle and space them as before, but stagger them so that they lie between the snips in the first seam allowance.

5 Lay the seam over a tailor's ham and press the seam allowances open. Then turn the fabric right side out along the seam and press the seam flat.

Left: an inward curve.

Outward curve

With this curve the seam allowances need to squash up, so notches need to be cut to let them do this without making lumps in the fabric.

1.

2.

3.

4.

5.

1 Follow Steps 1–2 of Inward Curve to sew the seam and trim the seam allowances.

2 Cutting at an angle, snip into one seam allowance, snipping down to about 3mm (⅛ in.) from the stitching.

3 Cutting from the other direction, snip down to the tip of the first cut to cut out a tiny triangle of fabric. Make notches in this way right along the curve, spacing them about 2cm (¾ in.) apart.

4 Notch the other seam allowance in the same way, but stagger the notches so that they lie between those in the first seam allowance.

5 Turn the fabric right side out along the seam and ease and press it with your fingers to make the seam lie along the edge of the curve. Then press the seam flat.

Right: an outward curve.

Tight curves

For a tight curve, you may not be able to turn the fabric enough under the presser foot. With the needle down, lift the foot at regular intervals and pivot the fabric a little, similar to a square corner.

Check out...

Stitches, page 23
How to run a sewing machine, page 21
Pinning, page 24
Pressing, pages 26–27
Sewing straight lines, page 30
Starting and finishing sewing, page 31
Open seam, page 34
Inward curve, page 68

Best used for...

All fabrics

Scallops

These are a mix of inward corners and outward curves and so require a combination of the techniques to make them perfect.

Check out...

Stitches, page 23

How to run a sewing machine, page 21

Pinning, page 24

Pressing, pages 26–27

Starting and finishing sewing, page 31

Inward square corner, page 66

Outward curve, page 69

Best used for...

Lightweight and mediumweight fabrics

Above: a scalloped edge.

1 Pin two pieces of fabric right sides together. Draw the scallops onto one of them; this pattern was made by drawing around a plate, overlapping each curve. Set the sewing machine to a medium straight stitch and machine-sew along the line. Lift the foot and pivot the fabric at the inward corners.

2 Cut out the scallops, cutting 1cm (⅜ in.) outside the stitching.

3 Snip into the inward corners. Notch the outward curves. Turn the scallops right side out along the seam and ease them into shape with your fingers. Press the seam.

Points

These are tightly angled outward corners, but they do need a slightly different treatment to make them lie neatly.

Check out...

Stitches, page 23

How to run a sewing machine, page 21

Pinning, page 24

Pressing, pages 26–27

Starting and finishing sewing, page 31

Outward square corner, page 67

Best used for...

Lightweight and mediumweight fabrics

Above: a point.

1 Follow Step 1 of Outward Square Corner to mark the end of the seam, then sew the first side. Lift the foot and pivot the fabric to make one stitch across the tip of the point. Pivot the fabric again to sew the second side of the point.

2 Trim the seam allowances as shown. Cut off the tip of the point 3mm (⅛ in.) from the stitching, then cut each side at an angle, following Steps 3–4 of Outward Square Corner.

Darts

These are little, angled pleats that shape fabric so that it lies smoothly around our curves. Well-sewn darts will make a good deal of difference to the fit of a garment.

Best used for...

All fabrics

1 Draw the dart on the wrong side of the fabric. If you are taking it from a pattern, make a tiny hole in the tissue at the tip of the dart then press the fabric marker over the hole to mark the tip on the fabric. Mark the top points of the dart and use a ruler to join the dots and so draw the dart.

2 Push a pin into the line on one side of the dart and push it out on the other line, making sure the pin is straight.

3 Push the layers of fabric together along the pin, then pin along the line with the head of the pin facing towards the point of the dart. If the fabric is slippery or otherwise tricky to sew, then tack just outside the marked line.

4 Set the sewing machine to a medium straight stitch. Starting at the edge of the fabric, machine-sew the dart. As you get to the tip, angle the stitching slightly so that the last couple of stitches run almost parallel to the fold.

5 Pull both threads through to one side and knot them firmly to secure the stitching. Remove any tacking stitches.

6 Press the dart flat and then press it to one side. If it's a waist dart then press it towards the side seam, if it's a bust dart then press it downwards. If the dart is very wide or the fabric very thick, cut away some of the fabric within the dart, leaving 1 cm (⅜ in.) seam allowances.

Below: a dart.

On the edge

Bindings and trimmings have both practical and pretty aspects that make them great solutions to all sorts of sewing situations. Bind an edge to reduce bulk and add a pretty finishing detail at the same time, or slip a trimming into a seam for a couture touch.

Making bias strip and binding

You can buy ready-made bias binding, but it's available only in limited colours. If you make your own – which is easy to do – then you can match or contrast it with your project to produce binding that adds an aesthetic as well as practical touch. You'll need a bias binding maker, which can be bought inexpensively at a sewing shop. There are various ways of producing the initial parallelogram; this way is fabric-hungry, but it has the fewest number of seams and so is my preferred technique.

1.

2.

3.

4.

Bias and straight grain

Fabric is woven from two threads, the warp and the weft, that cross each other at right angles. When the fabric is cut along the line of either of these threads it is being cut on the 'straight grain'. When fabric is cut diagonally across the threads then it is being cut 'on the bias'. Bias-cut fabric is stretchier, clings more and frays less than straight-cut fabric.

Check out...

Stitches, page 23
How to run a sewing machine, page 21
Pinning, page 24
Pressing, pages 26–27
Sewing straight lines, page 30
Starting and finishing sewing, page 31
Open seam, page 34

Best used for...

Lightweight and mediumweight fabrics
Woven fabrics

Making bias strip

1 Cut a rectangle of fabric on the straight grain and lay it flat and right side up. Fold one short end up to match the upper long edge. A triangle of the wrong side of the fabric is visible, as shown.

2 Press the diagonal fold.

3 Open the fabric out flat again and cut along the pressed fold to cut off the triangle of fabric.

4 Repeat Steps 1–3 to fold over, press and cut off a triangle at the other end of the rectangle, folding it so that the pressed line will slope in the same direction as the first line to produce a parallelogram. The sloping ends are on the bias.

5.

6.

7.

8.

9.

10.

11.

5 Cut a template strip of card that is the width of the fabric needed to make the bias binding. The packaging of your binding maker should tell you what width to use. On the back of the fabric, lay the template against one sloping edge of the fabric and draw along the other side of it, drawing a line that runs from one straight edge to the other straight edge, parallel to the slope. Then lay the template against this drawn line and draw a second line in the same way. Continue drawing lines across the fabric until you reach the other sloping edge, cutting off any excess along the last drawn line.

6 Right sides together, bring the two straight edges together. At one sloping end, match the bias edge with the first drawn line, thus offsetting all the lines by one. Pin the straight edges together to form a tube.

7 Set the sewing machine to a medium straight stitch and machine-sew the pinned seam, taking a 1.5cm (⅝ in.) seam allowance.

8 Press the seam open. You have made a tube of fabric with one continuous drawn line spiralling around it.

9 Starting at one end, cut along the drawn line to produce a continuous strip of bias tape.

Making bias binding

10 Feed one pointed end of the bias strip into the binding maker and pull it through.

11 Slowly pull the binding maker backwards along the strip, pressing the folds flat as they emerge.

Right: handmade bias binding.

Decorative bias binding

To make the most of your handmade bias binding, apply it so that it's visible. Binding edges in this way means that there is no folded hem, so it's great for stiff or bulky fabrics. Binding is also a good finish for sheers as it avoids hemming issues and adds a little weight that can help the fabric hang better.

Check out...

Stitches, page 23
How to run a sewing machine, page 21
Pinning, page 24
Tacking, page 25
Pressing, pages 26–27
Sewing straight lines, page 30
Starting and finishing sewing, page 31

Best used for...

Straight and curved edges
Make from lightweight and mediumweight fabrics
Trimming all fabrics

1 Open out one folded edge of the binding. Right sides together, pin the binding to the fabric, matching the raw edges.

Left: decorative bias binding on the right side of the project (above) and on the wrong side (below).

2 Tack the binding in place, stitching to one side of the fold (see Avoiding Pinholes, opposite).

3 Set the sewing machine to a medium straight stitch. Position the fabric in the sewing machine so that the needle will start sewing precisely on the opened-out fold in the binding. You can check that it is positioned correctly by turning the handwheel to lower the needle until it just touches the fabric. Machine-sew along the fold, reversing at each end to secure the stitching.

4 Remove the tacking stitches and press the machine stitching flat. Fold the binding over the stitching so that it lies right side up and covers the raw edge of the fabric. Press the binding flat.

5 Fold the binding right over the raw edge of the fabric and to the wrong side. The free edge of the binding should just cover the line of stitching that shows on the wrong side (see inset). On the right side, pin the binding in place.

6 Position the fabric in the sewing machine so that the needle will start sewing precisely along the seam between the binding and the main fabric: this is called 'stitch in-the-ditch'. Machine-sew the binding in place, reversing at each end.

Hidden bias binding

With this method of binding an edge the binding itself is not visible, though the final line of stitching is. It's good for heavyweight fabrics, as you are avoiding a double fold, but not great for sheers because it tends to look odd. You can either make your own binding or, as it's not going to be seen, use a purchased bias binding, as here.

Check out...

Stitches, page 23

How to run a sewing machine, page 21

Pinning, page 24

Tacking, page 25

Pressing, pages 26–27

Sewing straight lines, page 30

Starting and finishing sewing, page 31

Decorative bias binding, page 76

Best used for...

Straight and curved edges

Make from lightweight and mediumweight fabrics

Trimming all fabrics except sheers

1.

2.

3.

Avoiding pinholes

If the fabric and binding don't mark when a pin is put in and taken out again, pin and tack the binding in place along the centre. If holes do show, pin and tack along the folded-out edge of the binding, as opposite.

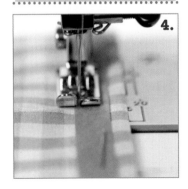

4.

1 Follow Steps 1–4 of Decorative Bias Binding to sew one side of the binding in place and press it over the edge of the fabric.

2 Fold the full width of the binding to the wrong side of the fabric, folding over a little of the fabric as well. The amount of fabric folded over can be as much or as little as required: here, enough was folded over to make the gingham pattern look neat on the right side. On the wrong side, pin the binding in place.

3 Press the folded edge of the fabric, avoiding pressing the pins.

4 Position the fabric in the sewing machine so that the needle will start sewing close to the free edge of the binding. Machine-sew the binding in place, reversing at each end to secure the stitching.

Right: hidden bias binding on the right side of the project (above) and on the wrong side (below).

Zigzag bias binding

This is a quick and easy binding technique, but it's not good-looking and so best reserved for neatening edges that won't be seen but that need to be well-finished. There is no need for a folded hem, so this is a good technique for bulky fabrics.

1.

2.

3.

4.

Check out...

Stitches, page 23
How to run a sewing machine, page 21
Pinning, page 24
Tacking, page 25
Pressing, pages 26–27
Sewing straight lines, page 30
Starting and finishing sewing, page 31
Finishing edges, page 32

Best used for...

Straight and curved edges
Hidden edges
Make from lightweight and mediumweight fabrics
Trimming all fabrics

Left: zigzag bias binding looks the same on both sides.

1 Fold the bias binding precisely in half and press it.

2 Slip the folded binding over the raw edge of the fabric, completely enclosing it. Pin the binding in place.

3 As it's a narrow edging, it's a good idea to tack the binding in place, especially if the fabric is slippery.

4 Set the sewing machine to a medium zigzag stitch. You can sew the binding in place in one of two ways, depending on the look you prefer and method you find easiest.

Turn the handwheel until the needle is as far to the right as it will go.

Position the fabric in the sewing machine so that the needle will start sewing on the binding, close to the edge. When the needle moves across to the left it will come down into the fabric, so the line of zigzag stitching will cover the join between the binding and the fabric. This method is used for the sample on the left

For the other method, set the machine up in the same way but position the fabric so that the needle comes down on the right close to the outer edge of the binding. When it comes down on the left it should be close to the edge overlapping the fabric, so the line of stitching lies entirely on the bias binding.

Remove the tacking stitches.

Shaping bias binding

Bias binding can be used on edges ranging from perfectly straight to tightly curved. However, if you are going to sew it to a curved edge you'll get a better finish if you shape it a bit first. You don't have to match the curve in the binding precisely to the edge being bound, but the nearer you get, the better.

Check out...

Stitches, page 23

How to run a sewing machine, page 21

Pressing, pages 26–27

Sewing straight lines, page 30

Decorative bias binding, page 76

Hidden bias binding, page 77

Zigzag bias binding, page 78

Best used for...

Curved edges

Make from lightweight and mediumweight fabrics

If the binding is going to enclose the edge, as for Decorative or Zigzag Bias Binding, fold the binding in half. For Hidden Bias Binding have it flat, as here. Press the iron down onto the binding close to one end, then pull the binding through under the iron, pulling it round to create a curve as you do so. How tightly round you pull the binding will dictate how tight the curve will be.

Right: bias binding shaped to a curve.

Straight binding

If the edge you are binding is straight, with no hint of a curve, then you can make the binding from fabric cut on the straight grain rather than on the bias. This is easier in that you just have to cut strips of fabric rather than create the bias parallelogram, but the techniques for applying it are exactly the same as for bias binding.

Check out...

Stitches, page 23

How to run a sewing machine, page 21

Pressing, pages 26–27

Sewing straight lines, page 30

Making bias strip and binding, pages 74–75

Decorative bias binding, page 76

Hidden bias binding, page 77

Zigzag bias binding, page 78

Best used for...

Straight edges

Make from lightweight and mediumweight fabrics

Trimming all fabrics

Right: a straight-bound edge using the Decorative Bias Binding technique.

Binding a corner

Using bias binding to trim neat, square corners is not difficult as long as you sew, measure and fold accurately. It's a good way of trimming place mats made from heavyweight, heatproof fabric.

Best used for...

Square corners

Make from lightweight and mediumweight fabrics

Trimming all fabrics

1.

2.

3.

4.

5.

6.

Left: a bound corner.

1 Follow Steps 1–2 of Decorative Bias Binding to tack the binding in place along one side of the corner. Measure back half the folded width of the binding from the corner and put in a pin to mark the spot. Position the fabric in the sewing machine so that the needle will start sewing precisely on the opened-out fold in the binding. Machine-sew along the fold as far as the pin, reversing at each end to secure the stitching.

2 Take out the pin and fold the binding straight up so that the fold lies diagonally across the corner.

3 Lay a ruler along the edge the binding is sewn to, matching it to the raw edges of the fabric and binding. Fold the binding straight down over the ruler so that the opened-out edge is matched to the raw edge of the fabric on the second side of the corner. Pin this edge in place.

4 Starting from the very top, at the folded-over edge, sew the binding to the fabric along the second side. Sew on the fold as before.

5 Turn the binding right side out over the corner of the fabric. It should turn easily and need minimal coaxing to form a perfect mitre.

6 On the back, fold the binding over to cover the visible lines of stitching and arrange the corner as neatly as possible. Follow Step 6 of Decorative Bias Binding to finish the binding, pivoting the fabric around the needle at the corner.

Piping

Piping is set into a seam and is sometimes thought of as a rather old-fashioned technique, but that's only true if the project and fabric you use are dated. Use piping to emphasise an outline shape, in a vivid colour to add an accent or in patterned fabric to create detail in an otherwise plain project.

Check out...

Best used for...

Straight and curved edges and seams

Make from lightweight and mediumweight fabrics

Trimming all fabrics

1 Make bias strip wide enough to encircle the piping cord plus 3cm (1¼ in.). Right side out, wrap the piping around the cord, matching the long raw edges and leaving a tail of cord protruding at each end. Tack the layers of fabric together, stitching close to, but not tight against, the cord. Note that this fabric has a diagonal check pattern, so when cut on the bias the pattern looks square.

2 Lay the piping on the right side of one piece of fabric, matching the raw edges. Pin the piping in place.

3 Set the sewing machine to a medium straight stitch and fit a zip foot. Position the fabric in the sewing machine with the side of the foot tight against the cord. Machine-sew the piping in place, reversing at each end to secure the stitching.

4 Lay the piped piece of fabric on top of the other piece, matching the raw edges. Pin the layers together.

5 Machine-sew as in Step 3, crowding the foot as tightly against the cord as possible so that this second line of stitching is a tiny bit closer to the cord than the first line. (If the first line of stitching is visible, your piping won't look very professional.)

Right: piping can be set into an edge seam (above) or an open seam within a project (below).

In-seam trimming

Setting fancy trimmings into a seam is a fabulous and easy way of adding decorative detail to a simple project. You need a trimming fit for the purpose – with one flat, stable edge that can be sewn into the seam – and there are literally thousands to choose from.

1.

2.

3.

4.

5.

6.

Check out...

Stitches, page 23

How to run a sewing machine, page 21

Pinning, page 24

Tacking, page 25

Pressing, pages 26-27

Sewing straight lines, page 30

Starting and finishing sewing, page 31

Open seam, page 34

Best used for...

Straight and curved edges and seams

Trimming all fabrics

Left: a trimming can be set into an edge seam (above) or an open seam within a project (below).

1 Using a fabric marker and a seam gauge to measure accurately, mark the 1.5cm (⅝ in.) seam allowance on one of the pieces of fabric.

2 Pin the trimming to the right side of the fabric with the flat edge just over the marked line, towards the raw edge.

3 Tack the trimming in place, stitching through the flat edge. After finishing the tacking, fold the seam allowance to the wrong side to check that none of the flat part of the trimming shows beyond the marked line.

4 Lay the other piece of fabric right side down on top of the trimmed piece, matching the raw edges. Pin the layers together.

5 Set the sewing machine to a medium straight stitch. Sew the seam, taking an accurate 1.5cm (⅝ in.) seam allowance.

6 If the trimming is to protrude from an edge seam, fold the fabric along the seam and very carefully press the fold only to avoid crushing the trimming.

Edge trimmings

As well as trimmings designed to be set into a seam, there are many, many other types and styles of trimming that work well sewn to the edge of a project. Here are just a few examples with information on how best to sew them on.

Check out...

Stitches, page 23

How to run a sewing machine, page 21

Pinning, page 24

Tacking, page 25

Pressing, pages 26–27

Sewing straight lines, page 30

Starting and finishing sewing, page 31

Best used for...

Straight and curved edges and seams

Trimming all fabrics

Choosing trimmings

There are some practical aspects to think about when choosing a trimming for a project. The trimming and fabric should have the same laundering requirements: a dry-clean only trimming on a cotton dress isn't a good idea. Also, the trimming can't be too heavy for the fabric or the project won't hang properly. A little weight can be good, but a chunky, beaded trimming on a floaty fabric won't work.

Do think about how you are going to attach a trimming before just machine-sewing it on across the middle. This trimming already had a line of machine stitching attaching the ruffled section to the velvet ribbon, so another line on the opposite edge of the ribbon looked fine. However, insensitive machine-sewing can spoil a trimming and some may be best attached using tiny hand stitches.

Some trimmings that aren't designed to be sewn into a seam will, in fact, work well when used that way. This sample shows wide ric-rac set into an edge seam, producing a delicate scallop.

The visible line of stitching needed to hold up a hem can detract from a pretty trimming, but this isn't a problem on faced edges. This daisy trimming is positioned half on, half off the fabric to add shaped detail to the edge. A line of stitching very close to the edge of the fabric holds the trimming in place and understitches the facing at the same time, preventing it rolling forwards.

An edge with a narrow hem can be detailed with flat braid that has at least one shaped edge that protrudes beyond the fabric. Sew it on with a line of machine stitching that holds the braid in place and the hem up at the same time. Do make a small test sample because a double hem topped by braid can be very chunky.

Fancy that

You, and your sewing machine, can produce gorgeous, decorative details that will add a glamorous touch to the most straightforward sewing projects. None of these techniques are difficult to master, though you will find that you have more choices to make than you do with purely practical techniques.

Gathered ruffle

An easy-to-make, feminine detail that looks great on women's and girl's garments alike. Made from crisp cotton they have a charming retro feel, while in filmy organza they are wonderfully romantic.

1.

2.

3.

Above: a gathered ruffle that has been set into an edge seam.

4.

How much ruffle?

Before you make miles of ruffles for a project, make some samples to see how the fabric gathers up and to decide how much you'll need. Twice the desired length, as used here, produces a soft ruffle in cotton, but in fine, sheer fabric you will probably need at least three times the length to make a ruffle that has any body to it.

Check out...

Stitches, page 23
How to run a sewing machine, page 21
Sewing straight lines, page 30
Starting and finishing sewing, page 31
Double hem, page 43
Narrow hem, page 43

Best used for...

Lightweight and mediumweight fabrics

1 Cut a strip of fabric twice the desired length of the ruffle, by the depth plus 2.5cm (1 in.): this is enough to make the hem and set the ruffle into a seam at the top. Using either the Double Hem technique (for cotton fabric) or the Narrow Hem technique (for sheer or silky fabric), make a 5mm (¼ in.) double hem along one long edge, which will be the bottom of the ruffle. If the short ends are going to be visible, hem them, too.

2 Set the sewing machine to a long straight stitch and loosen the tension. Position the fabric right side up in the sewing machine with the edge of the presser foot against the top raw edge. Sew right along the top edge, without reversing at the beginning or end of the stitching.

3 Starting at one end, pull gently on the bobbin thread to start gathering the fabric. Keep pulling, easing the gathers along to the middle. When you have gathered about half the ruffle, knot the threads and start

gathering from the other end. Pull and ease the gathers along gently: if you break the thread you'll have to start again. Once the ruffle is gathered up to the required length, knot the second set of threads.

4 Set the sewing machine to a medium straight stitch and set the tension correctly for the fabric. Taking a 1cm (⅜ in.) seam allowance, sew along the top of the ruffle, sewing the gathers down to stop them shifting about. Sew slowly and use your fingers to keep the gathers feeding evenly under the needle rather than bunching up into clumps. Reverse at each end to secure the stitching.

Knife pleats

These are my favourite style of pleat as they are quick to make and look great almost anywhere. Put them into the seam along the edge of a cushion, add them to the top of a bag or the bottom of a dress – anywhere they'll fit. The pleats are best made from fabric with a little body to it or they become floppy and the effect is lost.

1.

2.

3.

Above: knife pleats that have been pressed and set into an edge seam.

4.

Check out...

Stitches, page 23

How to run a sewing machine, page 21

Pinning, page 24

Sewing straight lines, page 30

Starting and finishing sewing, page 31

Double hem, page 43

Narrow hem, page 43

Gathered ruffle, page 86

Best used for...

Mediumweight fabrics

1 Follow Step 1 of Gathered Ruffle, but cut the strip of fabric three times the desired length. Along the top edge, measure and mark out the pleats on the right side of the fabric. They can be between 1.5cm (⅝ in.) and 3cm (1¼ in.) wide: any narrower and they resemble gathers and any wider and they loose their crispness. These pleats are 2cm (¾ in.) wide, so the little marks are that distance apart right along the top edge of the strip.

2 Right side up, pleat the fabric along the marked edge. Each pleat works over three marks: you pinch the fabric at the first mark, fold it over at the second mark and then bring the first mark down to touch the third mark. Repeat with the next group of three marks. Put a vertical pin in each pleat as you make it, with the head of the pin against the top edge of the fabric.

3 Set the sewing machine to a medium straight stitch. Taking a 1cm (⅜ in.) seam allowance, sew across the tops of the pleats to hold them in place. Sew slowly, taking out the pins as you get to them rather than sewing over them. Reverse at each end to secure the stitching. You can press the finished pleats for a crisper effect or leave them soft, as you prefer.

4 Even with the pleats pinned, it's easy for the toe of the presser foot to just slip underneath the edge of a pleat and fold it over, as shown, so keep a careful eye on what's happening. If you're at all concerned, take the extra time and tack the pleats using small stitches.

Box pleats

These are slightly more complicated pleats to make, but they do look beautiful and are very versatile. You can make a narrow band of them, as here, to use as a trimming, or you can add them to an existing garment pattern: you need to be quite confident in your sewing to do this.

Above: box pleats that have been pressed and set into an edge seam.

Check out...

Stitches, page 23

How to run a sewing machine, page 21

Pinning, page 24

Pressing, pages 26–27

Sewing straight lines, page 30

Starting and finishing sewing, page 31

Double hem, page 43

Narrow hem, page 43

Knife pleats, page 87

Best used for...

Mediumweight fabrics

1 Follow Step 1 of Knife Pleats to cut and hem the fabric. Box pleats can be almost any width; here they are 8cm (3 in.) wide. For pleats this width, measure and mark on the wrong side of the fabric 2cm (¾ in.) from one short end. Then make marks alternately 8cm (3 in.) and 4cm (1½ in.) apart, ending with a 8cm (3 in.) mark and a final 2cm (¾ in.) of fabric.

2 Wrong side up, pleat the fabric along the marked edge. These pleats work over two marks; simply match the first and second marks and put in a vertical pin, then repeat with every pair of marks. The pins will be sewing guides, so it's important that you put them in squarely. To check this, fold the fabric and put the head of the pin in where the two marks touch. Use a seam gauge to measure 4cm (1½ in.) from the fold and make sure the pin emerges at this measurement.

3 On the right side, starting about halfway down from the top edge, sew each pleat. This distance will vary depending on the effect you want. If you aren't sure, tack a few pleats first to see how they look. Position the fabric in the sewing machine at the required distance from the top edge with the needle in line with the tip of the pin. Reverse a few stitches,

then take out the pin and sew in a straight line to the marks on the top edge of the strip. Reverse to secure the stitching.

4 Lay the strip of pleated fabric right side up, so the stitched folds are facing you. Pinch the top of each fold to make a tiny crease, then flatten the fold, matching the crease to the line of stitching underneath. Put in a vertical pin on each side of the line of stitching to hold the box pleat flat.

5 To make sure the pleats are even and square before you sew them in place, press the bottom edge of each one. Adjust the fabric, re-pinning if necessary, to make each pleat lie flat next to its neighbour.

6 Follow Step 3 of Knife Pleats to sew across the top edge of the box pleats.

Pintucks

This is a technique that can be used almost anywhere to create a lovely vintage look. Garments of all sorts, bags, cushions, scarves, bed linen…anything made from a fairly crisp, lightweight to mediumweight fabric can benefit from the addition of a few pretty pintucks. You can make pintucks in sheer and floaty fabrics, but it's not that easy and I would recommend tacking before machine-sewing.

Above: pintucked silk fabric.

Check out…

Stitches, page 23
How to run a sewing machine, page 21
Pressing, pages 26–27
Sewing straight lines, page 30
Starting and finishing sewing, page 31

Best used for…

Lightweight and mediumweight fabrics
Fabrics with a crisp finish

1 Make and press a fold in the fabric 2cm (¾ in.) from the edge, making sure the fold is parallel to the edge.

2 Open the first fold out flat. Using a seam gauge to measure accurately, make and press another fold 2cm (¾ in.) from the first fold and parallel to it. Continue making folds in this way until a fold has been made for each pintuck required.

3 Set the sewing machine to a medium straight stitch. Starting with the last fold made, position the fabric in the sewing machine so that the needle will start sewing very close to the folded edge. You won't be able to use the marks on the throat plate to guide you, so choose another point on the machine bed to line up the edge of the fabric with: here, it is the inside edge of the right-hand feed dog. Machine-sew along the fold, reversing at each end to secure the stitching.

4 Move along to the next fold and repeat Step 3. Continue until each fold has been stitched and all the pintucks have been made.

5 Press all the pintucks flat, pressing them in whichever direction you prefer.

Sewing on ribbon or braid

Fabulous for dressing up a project or customising a garment, these trimmings aren't difficult to sew on, but do practise sewing straight lines.

Above: sewn-on ribbon.

Check out...

Stitches, page 23

How to run a sewing machine, page 21

Pinning, page 24

Tacking, page 25

Sewing straight lines, page 30

Starting and finishing sewing, page 31

Best used for...

All fabrics

1 Pin then tack the ribbon or braid to the fabric in the desired position. Tack a little way in from the edges.

2 Set the sewing machine to a medium straight stitch. Position the fabric in the sewing machine so that the needle will start sewing very close to the edge of the ribbon: the closer the better. You won't be able to use the marks on the throat plate to guide you, so you really need to concentrate on keeping the fabric running straight. The tricks are to sew slowly and to watch the position of the edge of the presser foot, not the needle because the up-and-down motion will distract you. Machine-sew along the ribbon, reversing at each end to secure the stitching.

3 Starting at the same end of the ribbon as for the first line of stitching, sew along the other edge in the same way. It's important to start at the same end each time as close rows of stitches running in opposite directions can distort the fabric and then the ribbon won't lie flat.

Sewing on ric-rac

This is one of the cutest trimmings there is and it gives a great retro look to children's and adults' garments alike.

Check out...

Stitches, page 23

How to run a sewing machine, page 21

Pinning, page 24

Tacking, page 25

Sewing straight lines, page 30

Starting and finishing sewing, page 31

Best used for...

All fabrics

Below: sewn-on ric-rac.

1 Pin then tack the ric-rac to the fabric. Tack along one edge, making a stitch through each scallop.

2 Set the sewing machine to a medium straight stitch. Position the fabric in the machine so that the needle will start sewing along the centre of the ric-rac. Check where one edge of the presser foot is in relation to the scalloped edge. Start to machine-sew very slowly, keeping the edge of the presser foot in the same place in relation to the scallops. If you try to watch where the needle is going, the up-and-down motion combined with the zigzagging of the ric-rac will have you sewing a wobbly line almost immediately.

Sewing on lace

Delicate and romantic, lace can be sewn on as an edging or it can be inserted into fabric using this technique. The gorgeous, very professional-looking, result is surprisingly easy to achieve. It's always worth making a test sample using the project lace and fabric to check that it looks as you hoped it would and that the lace works with the weight of the fabric. The technique is shown here with straight-edged lace, but it works equally well with a shaped edge.

Above: inset lace.

Check out...

Stitches, page 23

How to run a sewing machine, page 21

Pinning, page 24

Tacking, page 25

Sewing straight lines, page 30

Starting and finishing sewing, page 31

Sewing on ribbon or braid, page 90

Best used for...

Lightweight fabrics

1 Pin the lace in the desired position on the fabric.

2 Lay the fabric (and pinned-on lace) right side down. Using the backs of the pins as a guide, lay a strip of tear-away stabiliser, cut a little wider than the lace, over the back of the fabric where the lace is pinned on.

3 On the right side, tack through all the layers, stitching a little way in from the edges of the lace. Then take out all the pins.

4 Set the sewing machine to a narrow, tight zigzag stitch. Position the fabric in the machine so that the needle will start sewing close to the edge of the lace: the precise position will depend on the nature of the edge of the lace. This lace has a very delicate fringe, so the stitching lies just inside that. You can check that it is positioned correctly by turning the handwheel to lower the needle until it just touches the lace and then continuing to turn it to make one complete zigzag stitch. Follow Steps 2–3 of Sewing On Ribbon Or Braid to machine-sew the lace to the fabric.

5 Lay the fabric right side down and carefully tear way the stabiliser from the stitching. You may need to use tweezers to get all the shreds out of the back of the stitches without pulling them too hard.

6 Using small, sharp embroidery scissors, VERY CAREFULLY cut away the fabric between the lines of zigzag stitching. Cut as close to the stitches as possible without actually cutting into them.

Above: a free-motion embroidered flower.

Free-motion embroidery

The steps below offer a simple introduction to the wide, and exciting, world of embroidery using your sewing machine, a world I hope you'll want to explore further. Do read the appropriate section in your sewing machine manual as different machines have different ways of setting up for free-motion embroidery. You will certainly have to drop the feed dogs and either fit an embroidery (sometimes called darning) foot or take the foot off completely. If you do the latter then you must be very careful not to sew your fingers. Move the fabric under the needle by holding the outer edge of the hoop, not by pushing the fabric with your hands.

Check out...

How a sewing machine works, page 10

Stitches, page 23

How to run a sewing machine, page 21

Best used for...

All fabrics

1 Using a fabric marker, draw a motif onto the fabric.

2 Lay the fabric on a piece of tear-away stabiliser the same size and fit both layers into an embroidery hoop. Fit them in so that the inner hoop in on top of rather than underneath the fabric.

3 Set the sewing machine to straight stitch with a stitch length of zero, drop the feed dogs and fit an embroidery foot. Position the fabric in the machine with the needle to one side of the motif. Turn the handwheel to take the needle down and up again, pulling a loop of the bobbin thread to the right side. Hold both threads to one side as you start stitching. After a few stitches you can cut them off.

4 As the feed dogs are disengaged, it's the speed and direction in which you move the hoop that controls the length and direction of the stitches. Hold the hoop on either side and move it so that the needle will start sewing on the motif. Slowly press the power pedal to begin stitching and move the hoop so the line of stitches follows the drawn line. You can go backwards and forwards to make the line thicker as desired.

Binding the hoop

Binding the inner ring of the embroidery hoop with thin, bias-cut fabric (see Making Bias Strip And Binding, page 74) allows it to grip the embroidery fabric better, with less risk of marking or otherwise damaging it. Just wrap the fabric strip very tightly around the ring, securing the end on the inside with a few small stitches.

Appliqué

There are various types of appliqué and the style shown here is that most often used with a sewing machine. As with free-motion embroidery (opposite), there is a wide range of techniques to explore further.

Check out...
Stitches, page 23
How to run a sewing machine, page 21

Above; an appliquéd heart motif.

Best used for...
All fabrics

1 Following the manufacturer's instructions, iron fusible webbing onto the back of a piece of fabric.

2 Using a pencil, draw the required motif onto the paper backing of the webbing. Remember that as you are drawing on the back, the shape will be reversed when seen from the right side: this matters if you are drawing, for example, letters or numbers.

3 Cut out the motif and peel off the backing paper.

4 Again following the webbing manufacturer's instructions, iron the motif onto the right side of the background fabric.

5 Set the sewing machine to a wide, tight zigzag; this is known as satin stitch. Turn the handwheel until the needle moves across to the right. Position the fabric in the sewing machine so that when the needle comes down on the right-hand side of the stitch, it will pierce the fabric just outside the edge of the motif. Sewing slowly, satin stitch right around the motif. If you need to pivot the fabric (for example, to turn a corner), stop sewing with the needle down in the fabric on the right-hand side of the stitch. Lift the presser foot and turn the fabric as needed, then continue stitching. In this way the stitched outline will remain smooth.

Patchwork

Machine-sewn patchwork is a huge subject and there are many, many specialist books detailing different techniques and block patterns. Here is a flavour of what can be achieved by simply arranging squares and sewing seams. The more accurately you cut, sew and match seams, the better the patchwork will look.

Above: a simple patchwork.

Check out...

Stitches, page 23

How to run a sewing machine, page 21

Pinning, page 24

Pressing, pages 26–27

Sewing straight lines, page 30

Starting and finishing sewing, page 31

Finishing edges, page 32

Open seam, page 34

Intersecting seams, page 39

Best used for...

Lightweight and mediumweight fabrics

1 Cut squares of different fabrics the required size plus 5mm (¼ in.) all around. Set the sewing machine to a medium straight stitch. Right sides together and taking 5mm (¼ in.) seam allowances (a patchwork foot with a 5mm (¼ in.) toe is very useful here), pin then machine-sew squares together to make a strip the desired length. Repeat the process to make as many strips as needed.

2 Trim the ends of the seam allowances at an angle, as shown.

3 Press the seams open.

4 Right sides together, pin the strips together, carefully matching the seams.

5 Taking 5mm (¼ in.) seam allowances, machine-sew the strips together to make a patchwork.

Quilting

As with patchwork, quilting on the sewing machine offers a wide range of possibilities and we have only the space to explore the basic principles here. But they are great principles and you can easily take them further. Remember to always test stitch tension on a sample made up of scraps of all the fabrics.

Above: simple quilted fabric.

Check out...

Stitches, page 23

How to run a sewing machine, page 21

Pinning, page 24

Tacking, page 25

Sewing straight lines, page 30

Starting and finishing sewing, page 31

Best used for...

Lightweight and mediumweight fabrics

1 You need a main fabric, wadding and backing, the latter two being up to 5cm (2 in.) larger than the main fabric. A wool wadding is used here. Layer the fabrics with the lining right side down, then the wadding (matching the raw edges), then the main fabric right side up and centred. Pin the layers together around the edges.

2 Starting at one corner, tack diagonally across to the opposite corner. Repeat in the other direction to form an X shape. Then tack a cross, working from the midpoint of one edge straight across to the midpoint of the opposite edge, and the same in the opposite direction. Take out pins as they become redundant. Finally, tack around the edges. This tacking may seem time-consuming, but it will stop the layers shifting around as you machine-sew and it is worth doing. However, if the project is very small (perhaps less than 20cm (8 in.) square), then a diagonal cross and the edge tacking may be enough.

3 To quilt a simple pattern of lines, start at the midpoint of one edge. Set the sewing machine to a medium straight stitch and thread it with machine quilting thread if required, though you can use a normal sewing thread. If you have a walking foot for quilting then fit it, otherwise use a straight presser foot. Machine-sew straight across the fabric, reversing just a few stitches at each end.

4 A quilting bar fits onto the presser foot and the width can be set as required. Position the fabric in the sewing machine so that the end of the bar sits on the first line of stitching. Machine-sew across the fabric, keeping the end of the bar running along the stitches. Continue in this way, machining a few lines across the fabric in one direction. Then turn the bar around and machine the same number of lines in the other direction. Continue in this way until the fabric is completely quilted.

Make me, make me!

Now that you can sew, what do you want to make? Your newly acquired skills and a little practice will let you create gorgeous garments, desirable accessories, fabulous soft furnishings and anything else you might want to sew. Here are some specially designed, easy-to-make projects to get you started in the wonderful world of sewing.

Zipped up

With its flattering flared shape and fashionable handkerchief hemline, this simple-to-make skirt suits – and will fit – all shapes and sizes. If you make the skirt length longer than mid-calf at the back, then the points of the hem may trail on the floor at the front, but other than that there are no specific dos and don'ts. The waist ease allows the top of the skirt to sit on the hips, which works best with the shape, and it can either lie with the V at the front, as shown, or on one hip. You can use any fabric you want, though heavyweight fabrics may not drape very well.

You will need...

1 piece of fabric measuring the desired skirt length at centre back plus 7cm (2¾ in.), by the circumference of your waist plus 2cm (¾ in.) ease plus twice the skirt length plus 7cm (2¾ in.). (For example, you want the skirt to be 65cm (25½ in.) at centre back so the fabric length will be 65cm (25½ in.) + 7cm (2¾ in.) = 72cm (28¼ in.). Your waist measures 71cm (28 in.), so the fabric width will be 71cm (28 in.) + 2cm (¾ in.) + 65cm (25½ in.) + 65cm (25½ in.) + 7cm (2¾ in.) = 210cm (82½ in.). You can join pieces of fabric using an open seam at centre back.)
Iron
Ironing board
Pins
Scissors
Seam gauge
Tape measure
Sewing machine
Sewing thread to match fabric
Hand-sewing needle
Tacking thread
A zip that is 6cm (2½ in.) shorter than the desired skirt length
Hook and eye fastening

Check out...

Stitches, page 23
How to run a sewing machine, page 21
Pinning, page 24
Tacking, page 25
Pressing, pages 26–27
Sewing straight lines, page 30
Starting and finishing sewing, page 31
Open seam, page 34
Double hem, page 43
Corner hem, pages 46–47
Centred zip, pages 52–53
Shortening a zip, page 57

Choosing a zip

Standard dress zips come in the widest range of colours, but if you can find a separating zip in the right colour you can use that instead. In that case, choose a zip that is 4cm (1½ in.) shorter than the skirt length. Don't machine-sew a section of the seam, just fit the zip using the Separating Zip method (see page 55). With some fabrics, such as denim, a metal zip can look cool.

1 Turn under, press and pin a double hem around all four edges of the fabric. Mitre each corner, following Steps 1–8 of Corner Hem, but do not machine-sew the hem at this stage.

2 Fold the fabric in half across its length and put in a pin on the fold: this is centre back. Measure half your waist circumference plus 1cm (⅜ in.) out to each side from the fold and put in pins: these mark the start of the zip. Drape the fabric around your waist, pinning it together at the start of the zip, and check that the waist is comfortable and that the skirt is the desired length.

3 Right sides facing, fold the fabric in half again. On the waist edge, open out the pressed hem above the mitred corner and pin the layers together along the second pressed fold of the double hem, pinning as far as the pins marking the start of the zip.

4 Put in horizontal pins 4cm (1½ in.) and 6cm (2¼ in.) from the corner. Set the sewing machine to a medium straight stitch. Machine-sew along the pressed fold between the pins, reversing at each end to secure the stitching.

5.

6.

7.

8.

5 Tack along the pressed fold from the end of the machine-sewn section to the pins marking the start of the zip.

6 Position the zip with the pull just below the marking pins: the end stop should be just within the machine-sewn section. Pin, tack and machine-sew the zip in place. Remove all tacking stitches.

7 Hand-sew the hook and eye fastening to the zip tape, just above the pull.

8 Machine-sew the double hem right around the fabric, pivoting neatly at the corners.

Sleep on it

Pillowcases are so easy to make and provide the perfect way of jazzing up a plain bed linen set. Make them in good-quality cotton (the kind sold for quilting is perfect) if you are going to actually sleep on them, and in any fabric you like if they are going to be purely decorative. You can also make a matching bed banner for a great finishing accent. This one is quilted with irregularly spaced lines for a contemporary, asymmetric look that complements the fabric pattern.

You will need...

For the pillowcase:

A piece of fabric measuring twice the pillow length plus 20cm (8 in.), by the width plus 3cm (1¼ in.)

Sewing thread to match the fabric

For the banner:

2 pieces of main fabric each measuring the width of your bed plus 40cm (16 in.), by the desired banner depth plus 3cm (1¼ in.) (You can join fabric using open seams to get pieces the right width.)

1 piece each of backing fabric and polyester wadding measuring 5cm (2 in.) larger all around than the main fabric

Tacking thread

Hand-sewing needle

Quilting thread darker than the main fabric

Sewing thread to match the main fabric

For both:

Seam gauge

Tape measure

Iron

Ironing board

Pins

Sewing machine

Scissors

Check out...

Stitches, page 23

How to run a sewing machine, page 21

Pinning, page 24

Tacking, page 25

Pressing, pages 26–27

Sewing straight lines, page 30

Starting and finishing sewing, page 31

Finishing edges, page 32

Open seam, page 34

Double hem, page 43

Quilting, page 95

Pillowcase

1 Set the sewing machine to a medium straight stitch and at one short end of the piece of fabric, make a double hem.

2 At the other end make a narrower double hem, turning under 1cm (⅜ in.) for each fold.

3 Measure the length of your pillow from the end with the standard double hem made in Step 1. Wrong sides together and raw edges matching, press a fold across the fabric at this measured length.

4 Turn the fabric right sides together and fold it at the pressed line, matching the raw edges again. Approximately 14cm (5½ in.) will extend beyond the double hem: fold this piece right side down over the double hem.

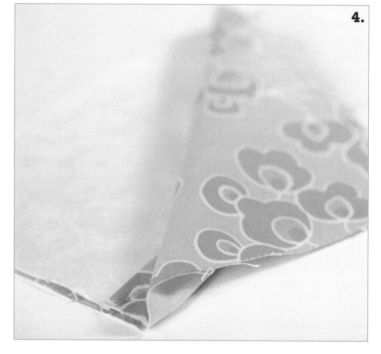

5 Pin the raw edges together; these are the side seams. Taking a 1.5cm (⅝ in.) seam allowance, machine-sew the side seams. Zigzag the seam allowances together. Turn the pillowcase right side out and press it.

Banner

1 Assemble the layers – the backing fabric right side down, the wadding and one piece of main fabric right side up. Tack a diagonal and a straight cross through all the layers, then tack around the edges.

2 Set the sewing machine to a medium straight stitch and thread it with the quilting thread. Roll up the banner as tightly as possible so that the roll will pass through the sewing machine to the right of the needle. Quilt a series of irregularly spaced vertical lines across the banner, sewing from one long edge straight across to the other one. If you have joined fabric then make sure that quilting lines run along the seam lines to hide them – this is called 'stitch in-the-ditch'. Remove the tacking stitches.

3 Right sides together, lay the second piece of main fabric over the quilted piece. Pin the layers together around the edges. Machine-sew around the edges taking a 1.5cm (⅝ in.) seam allowance and leaving a 15cm (6 in.) gap close to the end of one long edge. Zigzag the seam allowances together then trim off any excess wadding.

4 Turn the banner right side out through the gap. Press the edges and slip stitch the gap closed.

The classy cook

Be the complete domestic goddess with an apron that's so pretty you'll want to keep it on even when you're not in the kitchen. It's easy to make and doesn't need much fabric, so sew one to match every party outfit and be the most stylish cook in town. This version is trimmed with ric-rac, but you should choose a trimming to complement your fabric.

You will need...

1 piece of main fabric measuring half your waist measurement plus 26cm (10 in.), by the desired length of the apron plus 6cm (2¼ in.)

Fabric marker

Compasses or dinner plate

Scissors

Seam gauge

Iron

Ironing board

Pins

Enough medium ric-rac to go around the hemmed edges of the apron and around your waist plus 5cm (2 in.)

Hand-sewing needle

Tacking thread

Sewing machine

Sewing threads to match fabrics and ric-racs

2 pieces of contrast fabric and 1 piece of mediumweight iron-on interfacing each measuring your waist measurement plus 10cm (4 in.), 9cm (by 3½ in.)

Enough wide ric-rac to go around your waist plus 5cm (2 in.)

Template on page 127

28mm (1⅛ in.) self-cover button

Scrap of main fabric

Check out...

Stitches, page 23

How to run a sewing machine, page 21

Cutting out, page 25

Pinning, page 24

Tacking, page 25

Pressing, pages 26–27

Sewing straight lines, page 30

Starting and finishing sewing, page 31

Double hem, page 43

Outward curve, page 69

Curved hem, page 45

Automatic buttonhole, page 58

Box pleats, page 88

Sewing on ric-rac, page 90

Choosing fabric

If your apron is going to be as practical as it is pretty, then you must choose fabrics and trimming that can withstand the hot wash that may be needed to remove food stains. Quilting cotton is a good choice as it's got enough body to make a crisp apron.

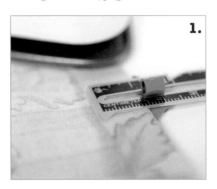

1 Round off the two lower corners of the main fabric: you can do this using compasses or by drawing around the edge of a dinner plate. Cut off the excess fabric. Turn under and pin a double 1.5cm (⅝ in.) hem down each side, around the curved corners and along the bottom edge.

2 Pin then tack the medium ric-rac around the turned-under edges. Set the sewing machine to a medium straight stitch and machine-sew the ric-rac in place, sewing the hem at the same time. Remove the tacking stitches.

3 In the raw top edge of the fabric, make two equally spaced box pleats. Each pleat uses 10cm (4 in.) of fabric and is positioned about 10cm (4 in.) in from a hemmed edge. Stitch 5cm (2 in.) down each pleat then open them out and tack across the top of them.

4 Iron the interfacing onto the back of one piece of the contrast fabric; this will be the inside of the waistband. Enlarge the template by 150% and cut it out to make a pattern. Fold the contrast fabric in half lengthways and pin the pattern to it with the short straight edge against the fold. Cut out the shape, extending it past the jagged lines to the edge of the fabric. Cut the same pattern out of the second piece of contrast fabric.

5 Press under 1cm (⅜ in.) along the long straight edge on both pieces of contrast fabric. Open the fold out flat again. Right sides together, pin the pieces to each other. Taking a 1.5cm (⅝ in.) seam allowance, machine-sew along the short sides and the top curved edge.

6 Turn the waistband right side out. Press the seam and re-press the fold along the long straight edge.

7 Make a buttonhole in one end of the waistband, positioning it horizontally and centrally.

8.

9.

10.

11.

12.

8 Pin, tack and machine-sew the remaining medium ric-rac along the top edge of the waistband. Fold it over at each end to neaten it.

9 Put in pins to mark the centre of the waistband and the centre of the apron section. Lay the waistband right side up and flat. Matching the pins, slip 1.5cm (⅝ in.) of the top of the apron between the pressed-under edges of the waistband. Pin the pressed edges of the waistband together right along their length, pinning the apron section in place as you go.

10 Machine-sew along the waistband, close to the pressed edges. Remove all tacking stitches.

11 Pin then tack the wide ric-rac over the stitching along the edge of the waistband. At the front, where the apron joins the waistband, shift the ric-rac down slightly to cover the join between the fabrics. Machine-sew the ric-rac in place, folding it over at each end to neaten it. Remove the tacking stitches.

12 Following the manufacturer's instructions, cover the button with the scrap of main fabric. Sew the button to the waistband to align with the buttonhole in the other end.

Shop til you drop

This eco-friendly, good-looking and easy-to-sew tote can be made in any sturdy fabric and to whatever size you need, just change the measurements as required. The enclosed and bound seams are strong and they keep the inside of the bag neat, so no fraying strands will entangle themselves around your purchases. Pick fabric to go with your coat for seriously co-ordinated grocery shopping.

You will need...

2 pieces of main fabric each measuring 35 x 38cm (14 x 15¼ in.)
Sewing machine
Sewing threads to match fabrics
Seam gauge
Iron
Ironing board
Pins
35cm (14 in.) of 2.5cm (1 in.) bias binding
Tape measure
2 pieces of main fabric each measuring 12 x 35cm (4¾ x 14 in.)
1 piece of contrast fabric measuring 67 x 7cm (26¾ x 2¾ in.)
Scissors
Hand-sewing needle

Check out...

1 Set the sewing machine to a medium straight stitch. Right sides together and using a mock French seam, sew the two large pieces of main fabric together along the long sides. Press the seams flat.

2 Making sure the side seams are at the sides and taking a 1.5cm (⅝ in.) seam allowance, sew across one short end of the fabric tube.

3 Press under 1.5cm (⅝ in.) at each end of the bias binding and press it in half along its length. Pin the binding across the seamed short end, over the seam allowance, and zigzag it in place.

4 Flatten out one corner of the bag, arranging it so that the side seam and base seam align on opposite sides of the point. Press the corner flat and pin it.

5 Measure 7cm (2¾ in.) along the side seam from the point and draw a line across the corner at right angles to the seam. Machine-sew along the drawn line, reversing at each end to secure the stitching. Sew the other bottom corner in the same way.

6 Hand-sew the points of the corners to the bound seam along the bottom of the bag.

7 Make a tie from each of the small pieces of main fabric, but do not turn under the short ends. These ties will be the bag handles.

8 Turn the bag right side out and lay it flat. Pin one end of a handle to the front of the bag, 8cm (3 in.) from the left-hand side seam and with the seam facing to the right. Match the end of the handle with the raw edge of the top of the bag.

Choosing fabric

I've used a traditional ticking fabric to make my shopping tote. Cotton duck, denim or canvas would also work well. If you are worried that the handles won't be strong enough to cope with all your purchases, slide a length of grosgrain ribbon between the folds before sewing the edges.

9 With the seam facing to the left (and making sure the handle isn't twisted), pin the other end to the front of the bag, 8cm (3 in.) from the right-hand side seam. Pin the other handle to the other side of the bag in the same way. Machine-sew back and forth over each end of each handle a few times, stitching 1cm (⅜ in.) from the edge. At this stage the handles will look as though they are sewn on upside down.

10 Join the short ends of the contrast strip using an open seam and zigzag the seam allowances. Press under 1.5cm (⅝ in.) along one edge.

11 Right sides together, matching the raw edges and matching the open seam to a bag side seam, pin the contrast strip to the top of the bag.

12 Machine-sew the contrast strip to the top of the bag taking a 1.5cm (⅝ in.) seam allowance. Trim and zigzag the seam allowances and understitch them as for a faced hem. Turn the contrast strip to the inside and press the top edge. The bag handles are now the right way up. Flatten the contrast strip against the inside of the bag and pin then machine-sew around the bottom edge.

Wrapped in ruffles

Shown here as an elegant evening accessory made in dupion silk, this versatile, simply designed wrap can have a very different feel in another fabric. Make it in lightweight woollen fabric as a glamorous extra layer in winter or in pretty cotton for a vintage-style cover-up to go with a summer dress.

You will need...

1 piece of fabric measuring
   16 x 350cm (6¼ x 140 in.) (this
   can be made by joining several
   smaller pieces using open seams)
Sewing machine
Sewing thread to match fabric
Seam gauge
Iron
Ironing board
Tape measure
2 pieces of fabric each measuring
   40 x 140cm (16 x 56 in.)
Compasses or dinner plate
Fabric marker
Scissors
Pins
Tacking thread
Hand-sewing needle

Check out...

Stitches, page 23
How to run a sewing machine,
   page 21
Pinning, page 24
Tacking, page 25
Pressing, pages 26–27
Sewing straight lines, page 30
Starting and finishing sewing,
   page 31
Finishing edges, page 32
Open seam, page 34
Outward curve, page 69
In-seam trimming, page 82
Gathered ruffle, page 86

Two-colour wrap

You can choose different colour fabrics for the two sides of your wrap. Remember that the ruffle will show on both sides in the same colour, so your choices do need to work well with each other. You can also choose different types of fabric, as long as they can be laundered together.

1.

2.

3.

4.

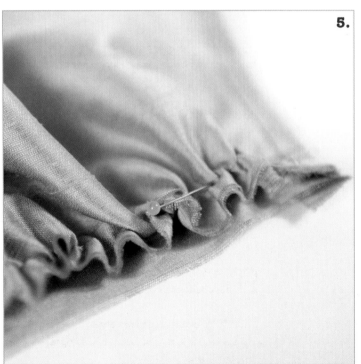

5.

1 Set the sewing machine to a medium straight stitch. On each short end of the long strip of fabric, make a 1cm (⅜ in.) double hem.

2 Set the sewing machine to a long straight stitch and loosen the tension. Fold the strip of fabric in half along its length, matching the two raw edges. Treating it as one layer of fabric, sew a line of gathering stitches along the edge. Don't forget to re-adjust the tension as soon as you finish the gathering.

3 Pull up the gathers until the strip measures approximately 200cm (80 in.) long.

4 Lay the large pieces of fabric on top of one another. Round off the two lower corners using compasses or by drawing around the edge of a dinner plate, then cut off the excess fabric. Press under 1cm (⅜ in.) along the top straight edge.

5 Right side up, lay one of the large pieces of fabric flat. Starting at one pressed top edge and matching the raw edges, pin the ruffle to the fabric.

6 Pin the ruffle around the curved edge of the fabric, finishing at the other end of the pressed top edge. Adjust the gathers to fit if needed. Tack the ruffle in place.

7 Right side down, lay the other large piece of fabric on top of the ruffled piece. Pin the pieces together around the ruffled edge.

8 Set the sewing machine to a medium straight stitch. Machine-sew the layers together, taking a 1.5cm (⅝ in.) seam allowance. Remove the tacking stitches, clip the curves, then zigzag the seam allowances together.

9 Turn the wrap right side out and carefully press the seam, being sure not to press and crush the gathers.

10 Match the pressed top edges and pin them together. Machine-sew them, sewing very close to the edge.

Tied up

Cushions are great projects for novice sewers – easy and quick to make, decorative to look at and not very fabric hungry. The steps are shown here are for a cushion with ribbon ties, but the same principles apply for the button and rouleaux loop variations.

You will need...

1 piece of fabric measuring
   30 x 100cm (12 x 39 in.)
4 lengths of 1.5cm (⅝ in.) grosgrain
   ribbon, each measuring 50cm
   (20 in.)
Tape measure
Pins
Seam gauge
Tacking thread
Hand-sewing needle
Sewing machine
Sewing thread to match fabric
Scissors
Iron
Ironing board
Cushion pad measuring 30 x 45cm
   (12 x 18 in.)

Check out...

VARIATIONS

A button-fastened cushion is made in the same way as a tie-fastened one, but make one hem deep enough to easily accommodate the buttonholes (you'll need to alter the length measurement of the fabric accordingly). Make the buttonholes, then fold the buttonhole end over first. Make up the cover and sew on buttons to match the buttonholes.

For a rouleaux fastening, you'll need to cut a facing piece of fabric. Make the loops and position them on one short end of the cover fabric. Sew the facing on, fold it to the back and press the seam. This end of the cover is folded over first. Make up the cover and sew on buttons to match the loops.

1 At one short end of the fabric, lay a piece of ribbon on the right side, 10cm (4 in.) in from and parallel to the edge. Match one raw end of the ribbon to the raw edge of the fabric. Position another length of ribbon in the same way, but placing it 10cm (4 in.) from the other edge. Pin the ribbons in place.

2 Fold a 1cm (⅜ in.) double hem, folding the ends of the ribbons into the hem as you do so. Tack the hem, making sure that the ribbons stay at right angles to the edge.

3 Set the sewing machine to a medium straight stitch. Machine-sew the hem close to the inner folded edge, then sew it again, close to the outer folded edge.

4 At the other short end of the fabric, machine-sew a 1cm (⅜ in.) double hem. Measure down 8cm (3 in.) from the hem. Pin the end of a piece of ribbon to the fabric at this point, positioning it 10cm (4 in.) in from and parallel to the raw edge. Position the final length of ribbon in the same way, but placing it 10cm (4 in.) from the other edge.

5 Set the sewing machine to a very narrow, tight zigzag stitch. Stitch across the end of a piece of ribbon, down one side for 1cm (⅜ in.), across the ribbon and then up the other side to the starting point. Sew on the other length of ribbon in the same way.

6 Roll up each ribbon and pin it to keep it out of the way. Right side up, lay the fabric flat. Measure 16cm (6¼ in.) from the end with the ribbons sewn into the hem and fold the fabric at this point.

7 Measure 30cm (12 in.) from the other end and fold the fabric at this point. This end will overlap the first folded end.

8 Pin the raw edges together. Machine-sew the seams taking 1.5cm (⅝ in.) seam allowances then zigzag the seam allowances together.

9 Turn the cushion cover right side out and press it. Insert the pad and tie the ribbons into bows. Trim the ends of the ribbons at an angle.

Put on the cuffs

Make this really pretty ribboned cuff in a colourway to go with your favourite party outfit: in fact, if you have sewn the outfit then use the same fabric for your cuff for the ultimate in co-ordinated jewellery. You only need little scraps of trimming, so raid your stash and add buttons and beads to your cuff if you wish.

You will need...

2 pieces of fabric and a piece of
    iron-on mediumweight interfacing
    each measuring the circumference
    of your wrist plus 2cm (¾ in.), by
    8cm (3 in.)
Scissors
Tape measure
Iron
Ironing board
Scraps of ribbons and ric-rac, each at
    least 8cm (3 in.) long
Seam gauge
Pins
Hand-sewing needle
Tacking thread
Sewing machine
Sewing threads to match fabric
    and ribbons
4 small eyelets
Eyelet setting kit
1 piece of organza ribbon measuring
    20cm (8 in.) long

Check out...

Stitches, page 23
How to run a sewing machine,
    page 21
Pinning, page 24
Tacking, page 25
Pressing, pages 26–27
Sewing straight lines, page 30
Starting and finishing sewing,
    page 31
Finishing edges, page 32
Open seam, page 34
Sewing on ribbon or braid, page 90
Sewing on ric-rac, page 90

1 Iron the piece of interfacing onto the back of one of the pieces of fabric; this will be the right side of the cuff.

2 Arrange the ribbons and ric-rac on the interfaced fabric, keeping them 2.5cm (1 in.) from the short ends. When you are happy with the arrangement, pin and then tack all the ribbons in place. If you want to overlap pieces of ribbon, as here, you will need to tack and machine-sew the lower layers before tacking the top layers.

3 Machine-sew each length of ribbon to the fabric. Remove the tacking stitches.

4 With right sides facing, lay the other piece of fabric on top of the beribboned piece, matching the raw edges. Pin the layers together.

5 Machine-sew around the edges, taking a 1.5cm (⅝ in.) seam allowance and pivoting at corners. Leave a 2.5cm (1 in.) opening in one short side.

6 Clip corners, trim off any protruding pieces of ribbon and turn the cuff right-side out.

7 Press the seams and slip stitch the gap closed.

8 Following the instructions on the eyelet kit, put two equally spaced eyelets into each short edge of the cuff, the spaces left free of ribbon in Step 2.

9 Lace up your cuff with a length of organza ribbon.

Choosing fabric

You need a lightweight fabric for this project. If you choose anything heavier, the additional bulk in the seams created by the interfacing and the ends of the ribbons and trimmings will result in very lumpy edges. Dupion silk, crisp cotton or fine-weave linen will all work well.

Glossary

I've made this book as jargon-free as possible, but there might be some terms that mystify you. Here is a list of the most commonly used and an explanation of what they really mean.

Appliqué A decorative technique where a shape is cut from one fabric and sewn onto another (see Appliqué, page 93).

Bias strip A strip of fabric that is cut at 45° to the straight grain. Such strips can be folded and made into bias binding (see Making Bias Strip and Binding, pages 74–75).

Clip To make small cuts into the seam allowance with the points of scissors (see Outward Curve, page 69).

Dart A stitched fold of fabric used to shape a garment (see Darts, page 71).

Facing A piece of fabric that is sewn to the main piece then turned to the back so that the seam allowances are hidden (see Rouleaux Loops, pages 62–63).

Feed dogs These are the 'teeth' that lie under the throat plate of the sewing machine and feed the fabric through it (see How A Sewing Machine Works, page 10).

Finishing edges Sewing or binding raw edges of fabric to stop them fraying (see Finishing Edges, page 32).

Fusible webbing This is heat-activated fabric glue that comes in a very thin sheet on a paper backing (see Appliqué, page 93).

Gathering Sewing a line of stitches along the edge of a piece of fabric, then pulling them tight to ruffle up the fabric (see Gathered Ruffle, page 86).

Hem allowance The amount of fabric that is folded over to make a hem. If more than one fold is made, then the hem allowance is the total amount of fabric needed to make all the folds (see Hem Allowance, page 42).

Interfacing A woven or knitted fabric that is used to support and stiffen areas of garments and other sewing projects. Fusible interfacing has one side covered with heat-activated glue and it can be ironed onto fabric (see Rouleaux Loops, pages 62–63).

Mitre An angled join at a square corner (see Corner Hem, pages 46–47).

Notch To cut small V-shapes into the seam allowance with the points of scissors (see Inward Curve, page 68).

Pivot To put the sewing machine needle down into the fabric, lift the presser foot and turn the fabric around the needle so you can start sewing in a new direction (see Inward Square Corner, page 66, and Outward Square Corner, page 67).

Presser foot The part of the sewing machine that holds the fabric flat against the feed dogs while it is being sewn. There are different presser feet for various sewing tasks (see Sewing Machine Accessories, pages 14–15).

Raw edge A cut edge of fabric that has not been finished by sewing or binding (see Finishing Edges, page 32).

Right side This is the side of the fabric that will be facing outwards on the finished project. It is sometimes abbreviated to RS.

Rouleaux A thin tube of bias fabric that is folded and sewn into a seam to make a loop (see Rouleaux Loops, pages 62–63).

Seam allowance The amount of fabric between the raw, cut edge and the line of stitching that makes the seam. In dressmaking the standard seam allowance is 1.5cm (⅝ in.), though you should always check a sewing pattern to see what it requires (see Sewing Straight Lines, page 30).

Selvedge The edge along the length of the fabric that is created during production and won't fray (see Single Hem, page 42).

Sheer fabric Fabric that is translucent.

Stabiliser A product that is laid on the back of fabric to support it while it is being worked on. Once the work is complete, the stabiliser is removed. There are various different types suitable for different tasks and fabrics (see Sewing On Lace, page 91, and Free-motion Embroidery, page 92).

Straight grain The directions that the threads that make up the fabric run in. The warp runs lengthwise and the weft runs widthwise. When the fabric is cut along the line of either of these threads it is being cut on the 'straight grain'. When it is cut on the weft this is sometimes called being cut on the 'cross grain'.

Tacking Sewing layers of fabric together to hold them temporarily until the final sewing is complete (see Tacking, page 25).

Understitch To sew a line of stitches within the seam allowance to hold a facing flat (see Rouleaux Loops, pages 62–63).

Wrong side This is the side of the fabric that will be facing inwards on the finished project. It is sometimes abbreviated to WS.

Template

The Classy Cook, pages 106–109
Waistband template, enlarge by 150%

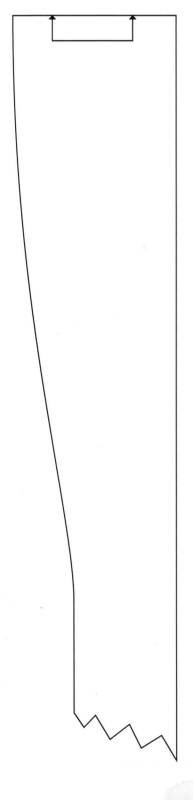

Resources

BOROVICK
www.borovickfabricsltd.co.uk
A great selection of unusual
and exciting fabrics, and really
great staff.

THE CLOTH HOUSE
www.clothhouse.com
Two branches, one selling
cottons and linens, the other
selling wools and fancy fabrics.
Both are just heavenly for fabric
fans, and they sell some lovely
buttons and trimmings as well.

FABRICS GALORE
www.fabricsgalore.co.uk
This is always my first stop
when I'm fabric shopping as
the selection and the prices are
so good.

JANOME
www.janome.com
The brand of sewing machine
and accessories that I use.

JOHN LEWIS
www.johnlewis.com
First stop for sewing equipment
and accessories.

KLEINS
www.kleins.co.uk
Trimmings, ribbons, buttons,
buckles and generally fab bits
and pieces; always worth a visit.

LIBERTY
www.liberty.co.uk
Beautiful things – the place to go
if you want really special sewing
notions. Plus a good range of
printed fabrics.

ROWAN
www.knitrowan.com
Some of the most interesting
and contemporary printed
fabrics around.

Acknowledgments

My thanks to Paula Breslich for commissioning this book and to Katie
Hardwicke for ensuring that it made sense. Dominic Harris took the
gorgeous step and style photographs and Louise Leffler was the brilliant
book designer. Laura Wheatly and Camilla Coburn Davis were the
glamorous models. And thanks, as always, to Philip for putting up with it all.

Index